# CAMBRIDGE

Sam Smith

# An Inspector Calls
## GCSE English Literature for AQA
### Student Book
Jon Seal
Series editor: Peter Thomas

# CAMBRIDGE
## UNIVERSITY PRESS

University Printing House, Cambridge CB2 8BS, United Kingdom

Cambridge University Press is part of the University of Cambridge.

It furthers the University's mission by disseminating knowledge in the pursuit of education, learning and research at the highest international levels of excellence.

www.cambridge.org
Information on this title: www.cambridge.org/9781107454552 (Paperback)
www.cambridge.org/9781107454606 (Cambridge Elevate-enhanced Edition)
www.cambridge.org/9781107454675 (Paperback + Cambridge Elevate-enhanced Edition)

© Cambridge University Press 2015

This publication is in copyright. Subject to statutory exception and to the provisions of relevant collective licensing agreements, no reproduction of any part may take place without the written permission of Cambridge University Press.

First published 2015

Printed in the United Kingdom by Latimer Trend

*A catalogue record for this publication is available from the British Library*

ISBN 978-1-107-45455-2 Paperback
ISBN 978-1-107-45460-6 Cambridge Elevate-enhanced Edition
ISBN 978-1-107-45467-5 Paperback + Cambridge Elevate-enhanced Edition

Additional resources for this publication at www.cambridge.org/ukschools

Cambridge University Press has no responsibility for the persistence or accuracy of URLs for external or third-party internet websites referred to in this publication, and does not guarantee that any content on such websites is, or will remain, accurate or appropriate. Information regarding prices, travel timetables, and other factual information given in this work is correct at the time of first printing but Cambridge University Press does not guarantee the accuracy of such information thereafter.

---

NOTICE TO TEACHERS IN THE UK

It is illegal to reproduce any part of this work in material form (including photocopying and electronic storage) except under the following circumstances:
(i) where you are abiding by a licence granted to your school or institution by the Copyright Licensing Agency;
(ii) where no such licence exists, or where you wish to exceed the terms of a licence, and you have gained the written permission of Cambridge University Press;
(iii) where you are allowed to reproduce without permission under the provisions of Chapter 3 of the Copyright, Designs and Patents Act 1988, which covers, for example, the reproduction of short passages within certain types of educational anthology and reproduction for the purposes of setting examination questions.

## Message from AQA

This textbook has been approved by AQA for use with our qualification. This means that we have checked that it broadly covers the specification and we are satisfied with the overall quality. Full details of our approval process can be found on our website.

We approve textbooks because we know how important it is for teachers and students to have the right resources to support their teaching and learning. However, the publisher is ultimately responsible for the editorial control and quality of this book.

Please note that when teaching the GCSE English Literature (8702) course, you must refer to AQA's specification as your definitive source of information. While this book has been written to match the specification, it cannot provide complete coverage of every aspect of the course.

A wide range of other useful resources can be found on the relevant subject pages of our website: www.aqa.org.uk

# Contents

## INTRODUCTION — 4

## INTRODUCING *AN INSPECTOR CALLS* — 6

## PART 1: EXPLORING THE PLAY

| Unit 1 | Home sweet home | 16 |
| Unit 2 | Confidence and conflict | 24 |
| Unit 3 | Rights and responsibilities | 32 |
| Unit 4 | Complaints and consequences | 40 |
| Unit 5 | Truth and lies | 48 |
| Unit 6 | Appearance and reality | 56 |
| Unit 7 | Duty and downfall | 64 |
| Unit 8 | Parents and problems | 72 |
| Unit 9 | Revelations and responsibility | 80 |
| Unit 10 | Ideas and attitudes | 88 |

## PART 2: THE PLAY AS A WHOLE

| Unit 11 | Plot and structure | 96 |
| Unit 12 | Context and setting | 101 |
| Unit 13 | Character and characterisation | 104 |
| Unit 14 | Themes and ideas | 108 |
| Unit 15 | Language | 113 |

## PREPARING FOR YOUR EXAM — 116

Glossary — 126

Acknowledgements — 127

# Introduction

Welcome to your AQA GCSE English Literature student book on *An Inspector Calls*. This is one of Priestley's best-known plays, and we hope you will enjoy it both at GCSE and later in life.

Much of the play deals with things that you are familiar with, and perhaps even an expert on – family loyalties, tensions, conflicts and being put on the spot for things you may have done in the past. It also includes ideas about what is wrong with society and what is needed to make it better.

This book will help you make the most of the play and of your GCSE. It will develop your skills in reading and responding to a modern drama text, and in writing for GCSE English Literature.

The book is organised as follows:

## Part 1: Exploring the play

Part 1 leads you through each act of the play. It ensures you build a thorough understanding of the action, dramatic structure and methods that Priestley uses to present his characters and ideas as a text to be performed to the audiences of *An Inspector Calls*.

Alongside text-based approaches, each unit provides activities for discussion and drama, with links to videos and other resources that will deepen your experience, understanding, interpretation and analysis of the play.

You will also develop your skills in writing about *An Inspector Calls*. Your work in each unit will result in notes and focused responses on aspects of the play that are important for GCSE. These will also be useful when you revise for your exam.

## Part 2: The play as a whole

Part 2 provides an overview of key aspects of the play, including structure, context, characterisation and language. It will develop your detailed knowledge and understanding, and also help you to revise your responses to the play as a whole.

## Preparing for your examination

This part gives you practice and guidance to help you prepare for your examination. It also provides examples of answers showing skills at different levels, so you can assess where your skills are strong and where to focus your efforts to improve.

## Working on Cambridge Elevate

As you work through this book you will find links to Cambridge Elevate, the Cambridge University Press digital platform. At these points, you are invited to complete a task, listen to an extract or watch a video to help you reinforce your learning.

 Watch a video when you see this icon.

 Complete an activity when you see this icon.

We hope that you will enjoy using these resources, not only to support your GCSE study, but to help you see that modern drama has plenty to say about the life around you – and within you.

*Peter Thomas*
*Series Editor*

# Introducing *An Inspector Calls*

## J.B. PRIESTLEY AND *AN INSPECTOR CALLS*

### Modern drama

Most people's experience of drama today comes from the television – from sitcoms and other shows. These programmes attract huge audiences and can run for years, with plots and characters developing and changing over time. Television programmes can also be digitally controlled: viewers can pause if they want to take a break or rewind if they miss something.

In contrast, *An Inspector Calls* is a one-off show lasting less than two hours. Audiences watch the whole play from start to finish (with perhaps one or two intervals). Live theatre also provides an experience that television cannot – it is always immediate and performances can vary from night to night. There are few distractions when watching a live performance in a dark theatre.

J.B. Priestley wrote in an era before television, although he was involved in early radio work. In Priestley's day, people went to the theatre for entertainment but, once there, a playwright could harness an audience's interest, curiosity and concentration to make them think.

### J.B. Priestley

John Boynton Priestley was born in 1894 and died in 1984, so his life covered events as diverse and dramatic as the First World War, the Russian Revolution, the General Strike, the Second World War, the first moon landing, the election of the first female prime minister in Britain and the rise of television as a medium of entertainment and information.

Priestley gained a lot of life experience before he became a successful writer. He left school at the age of 16 and worked as a junior clerk before serving in the army during the First World War. After the war he did a degree at Cambridge University, which led him into working for the BBC, writing books and plays, and then into politics. He believed that it was the government's job to protect the poor and stop them being exploited by the rich.

## An Inspector Calls

Priestley wrote *An Inspector Calls* in 1944-45, but it is set in 1912. The play comprises three acts (not divided into scenes), with six characters in a single setting. The story unfolds in real time.

## The ideas of the play

*An Inspector Calls* is a play with a strong sense of purpose. It is important to understand the links between the characters, the setting and the writer's purpose. These links often take the form of common themes and ideas.

**Themes** are the subjects that drama can be based on. The most common themes are love and hate in relationships, reactions to events large and small, and examples of human traits such as courage, doubt, fear, success and failure. The main themes of *An Inspector Calls* are responsibility and how an individual relates to others in society.

**Ideas** are ways of understanding aspects of the themes. Ideas about love, for example, can be that it makes the world and people better, or that it makes them insecure and jealous, or that it does not last, or that it helps people through difficult times. Ideas about war are that it can bring out the best in people or that it brings out the worst in them, that it is necessary to defend something important or that it is tragic because it is not necessary. One idea in *An Inspector Calls* is that living a life focused on material gain leads to a loss of responsibility and to conflicts between individuals and society.

A writer's ideas might include any of these things, but you should also consider whether ideas are represented by characters as a way of creating dramatic conflict, or if these are expressions of what the writer believes.

Priestley did not write his play simply as an entertainment. As a writer, there were things he wanted to say and issues he wanted to explore. His ideas about responsibility, for example, include a belief that capitalism makes society less fair. Here are some of the ideas that Priestley returns to in the play:

- responsibility and duty
- the difference between generations
- appearance and reality
- gender
- social class and establishment
- lies and secrecy.

 Read more about the themes and ideas in the play in Unit 14.

## Stagecraft

Priestley could have conveyed his ideas in a novel. He chose to write a play because he wanted his ideas to be immediately obvious to an audience that could see and hear them in action. In other words, he wanted to use the impact of drama in performance. As a playwright, Priestley makes it clear what he wants the actors to do on stage by giving them guidance in the stage directions.

## Theatricality

Performance is best when it involves surprise, variety and contrast. Surprise is a matter of plot. Variety can be to do with the mix of characters, emotions and attitudes, appealing to all possible tastes in the audience. Theatricality is the ability to fill an evening in the theatre with enough to keep the audience interested and entertained so they come back again.

## Interpretation

Your own response to the play matters – your opinion of the characters and which parts of the play make you think. Most important is what the play means to you when it shows you how people behave and how relationships develop or go wrong. Interpretation can be personal to you, or related to all people, or to some people.

## Language

In a modern play, the language is natural – sounding as much like ordinary speech as possible – rather than being presented in verse as it was in Shakespeare's day, for example. A playwright's skill is in writing a script that reflects the individual voices of the characters, using habits of speech and words that are characteristic of their mood, manner and motivation. For example Arthur Birling's speech is full of derogatory terms such as '**cranks**', assertions such as '**there isn't a chance of war**' and instructions and advice to others, such as '**I know**' and '**listen to me**'.

 Read more about language in the play in Unit 15.

> I say there isn't a chance of war.
>
> *Arthur Birling: Act One*

## Performance

Drama is a public entertainment. Whether on stage or screen or in your classroom, you will be closest to Priestley when you see the script in action. This is where your understanding of plot and character, themes and ideas, language, stagecraft and theatricality come together, because interpretation and performance are what the text is all about. Connecting the words with what actors have done, or with what you think actors could do with them, will ensure that you write about Priestley as a dramatist.

## Context

You need to know something about the times in which Priestley lived and wrote – mainly about the events he mentions: strikes, the situations in Germany and Russia, and the launching of the *Titanic*. This is not a history task; you simply need to know that Priestley uses these events to show Birling's opinions. The most important context is that of the society in which we live and the way that Birling's views – and those of the Inspector – relate to it.

There is also the context of performance – the different ways in which a scene may be performed on screen and on stage, for an audience of children or adults. You are studying the play in the context of GCSE English Literature, which may be different from the context of watching it in the theatre.

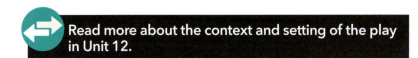
Read more about the context and setting of the play in Unit 12.

## MODERN DRAMA AND GCSE ENGLISH LITERATURE

Your GCSE English Literature course has been designed so that you experience a range of drama, prose and poetry texts from the last few hundred years. *An Inspector Calls* was first performed in the Soviet Union in 1945 and in London in 1946, and the play is set in 1912, so it is firmly placed as 20th-century drama.

Your GCSE English Literature exam has two papers: Paper 1 is Shakespeare and the 19th-century novel, which is worth 40% of your GCSE. Paper 2 is Modern texts and poetry, which is worth 60% of your GCSE.

Paper 2 – Modern texts and poetry – has three sections:

**Section A Modern texts:** this is where you answer one essay question from a choice of two on your studied modern prose or drama text – in this case, *An Inspector Calls*.

**Section B Poetry:** this is where you answer one question on comparing poems from your chosen cluster of the anthology, 'Love and relationships' or 'Power and conflict'.

**Section C Unseen poetry:** this is where you write about a poem that you have not seen before and then compare this poem with a second unseen poem.

## GCSE English Literature assessment objectives

The assessment objectives (AOs) form the basis for the GCSE mark scheme. You will be assessed on your skill in writing about what the play is about and how it is written. For Paper 2, Section A, you will be assessed against four assessment objectives:

**AO1:** Read, understand and respond to texts. Students should be able to:

- maintain a critical style and develop an informed personal response
- use textual references, including quotations, to support and illustrate interpretations.

**AO2:** Analyse the language, form and structure used by a writer to create meanings and effects, using relevant subject terminology where appropriate.

**AO3:** Show understanding of the relationships between texts and the contexts in which they were written.

**AO4:** Use a range of vocabulary and sentence structures for clarity, purpose and effect, with accurate spelling and punctuation.

## LITERATURE SKILLS AND STUDY FOCUS AREAS

Most of your study will be based on reading the text, but this will not be enough if you are to understand and enjoy the play as drama. You need to see that the text does not become drama until it is performed, and actors bring the words to life. So make sure that you see the play and connect the words on the page with performance on stage or screen.

Most of the skills you develop in your literature study will be the same as those in other parts of your GCSE English reading. You will develop your core skills to show understanding, interpretation and analysis. These skills, along with the following study areas, give a focus for your work in this book.

## Ideas, attitudes and feelings

Ideas, attitudes and feelings make up the content of the play. The important thing to remember is that they are three different things.

- **Ideas** are the thoughts that explain or result from an experience.
- **Attitudes** are the positions or postures adopted when facing experiences.
- **Feelings** are the emotions people feel, which are often quite different from their attitudes and ideas.

For example you could say that:

- an **idea** is that age and experience matter
- an **attitude** could be confidence in experience and age
- a **feeling** is anger at people who do not respect experience and age.

## The writer's methods

You will be expected to understand and respond to the feelings, ideas or attitudes expressed in the play, and also understand and respond to the way the play is written – the writer's methods. These amount to language, form and structure. These are also three different things. For example you could say that:

- the **language** shows a contrast between the formal language of Birling's generation and some slang terms of the younger people; you could also say that the language is characteristic of a character's mood, manner or motivation
- the **form** is a three-act play with no division into scenes
- the **structure** is based on a sequence of interrogations of characters by Inspector Goole.

## Developing written response skills

This book supports you in writing that is focused on the GCSE study areas. It helps you to identify where your skills are strong and what you need to do to improve. Develop your skills from 'basic' comments that are relevant and include a quotation to support the comment, to using your understanding and interpretation skills to explain feelings, motives or reasons and to include ideas that develop and extend meaning. For example:

**Understanding:** It is about what happens when an Inspector calls on a family who are celebrating an engagement and are pleased with themselves.

**Explaining:** It is about a family realising that they have all had a part in causing a tragic event, and reacting differently to discovering this responsibility.

**Conceptualising:** It is about the importance of seeing society as more than a capitalist jungle where each person looks after their own interests, and accepting that moral and social responsibility should matter more than profits.

## Writing with focus

This book also develops focused writing skills, so you can be ready and confident when writing in timed conditions in the exam. Be prepared to show how Priestley builds each character as a person in the play, uses his writer's craft to treat them as a dramatic device and as mouthpieces for his ideas. When you respond to a question on the play, you need to show that your response is dealing with essential skills and linked to specific details of the text. Make your points quickly and link your chosen textual detail to a clear purpose.

## THE ACTION OF *AN INSPECTOR CALLS*

### The plot

The play is set in 1912. The action takes place in the dining room of the Birlings' house. They are a wealthy upper middle-class family, who have gathered to celebrate the engagement of the daughter Sheila to Gerald, a young man from an aristocratic family.

Mr Birling is very pleased with the world and particularly his own achievements. He is delighted that his daughter is marrying into the aristocracy and sees this as a mark of his own success.

But all is not what it seems. Into this cosy and comfortable evening comes Inspector Goole. He is investigating the death of a young woman, Eva Smith. At first the family are frustrated that their celebrations have been interrupted. However, as the evening proceeds the characters all find themselves involved and, one by one, they confront the parts they have each played in the girl's suicide.

The Inspector's questioning forces each character to reflect on their own actions and the effect these have on others. The older members of the family find this threatening and they resist. For some of the younger characters, the evening marks the start of change.

Like all good literature, *An Inspector Calls* reaches across time – from its 1912 setting to its original post-Second World War audiences and right on to the present day.

 Read more about the plot and structure of the play in Unit 11.

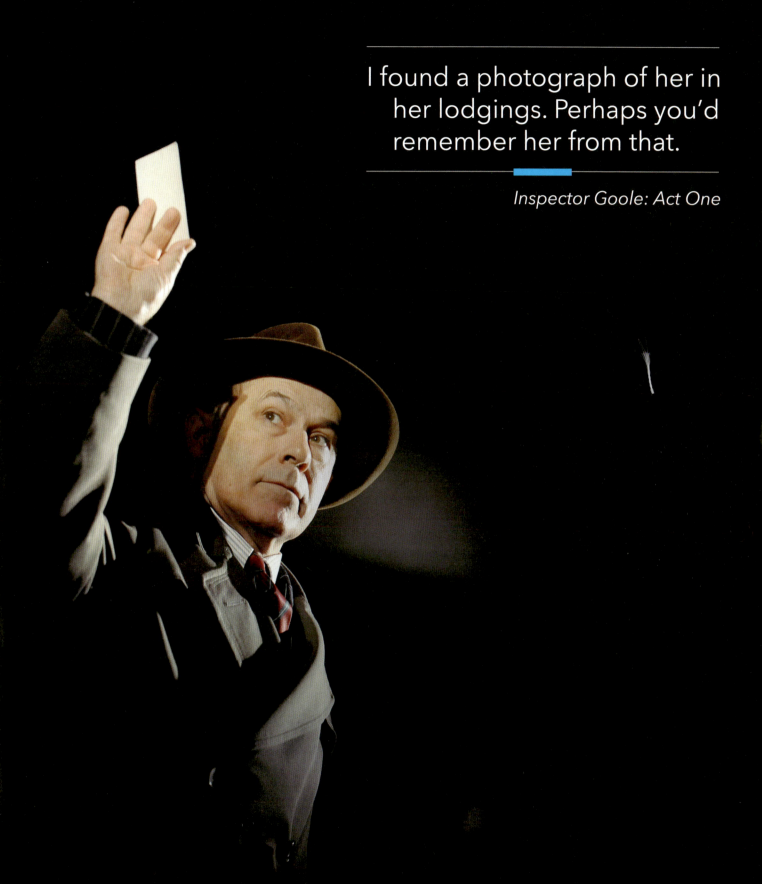

Introducing An Inspector Calls

> I found a photograph of her in her lodgings. Perhaps you'd remember her from that.
>
> *Inspector Goole: Act One*

# GCSE English Literature for AQA: An Inspector Calls

## THE CHARACTERS IN *AN INSPECTOR CALLS*

### Arthur Birling

Mr Birling is the father of Sheila and Eric. He is married to Sybil (Mrs Birling). He is a successful businessman who has been a mayor and magistrate.

### Sybil Birling

Sybil Birling is married to Arthur and is the mother of Sheila and Eric.

### Sheila Birling

Sheila is the daughter of Arthur and Sybil Birling. She is sister to Eric and is engaged to Gerald.

### Eric Birling

Eric is the son of Arthur and Sybil Birling, and brother to Sheila.

### Gerald Croft

Gerald is engaged to Sheila. He is the son of Birling's business rival, who is a man of high social status.

## Inspector Goole

Goole is the mysterious inspector who calls to question the characters. The audience is left without answers about his background and identity.

## Edna

Edna is the maid of the Birling's household in a time when Edwardian society was divided into classes and servants waited on the wealthy.

## Eva Smith

Eva is a young woman in her early twenties who has taken her own life. Eva is not a character on stage. However, her presence is central to the play, to each of the characters and to the Inspector's investigation.

Read more about character and characterisation in the play in Unit 13.

# 1

## Home sweet home

### How does Priestley present the opening and the character of Sheila?

Your progress in this unit:
- explore how Priestley opens the play
- understand and explain the character of Sheila at the start of her journey
- understand the characters at the start of the play and their relationships with Sheila
- explore the way Priestley presents characters to an audience
- develop a response to writing tasks.

## GETTING STARTED – THE PLAY AND YOU

### A suitable marriage

1. Imagine you have a friend from a very privileged background. You are worried that their upbringing has made them spoilt and naïve. They are about to get married, but you know that the person they are about to marry is not all they seem to be. Write down the conversation you would have with them as a short play script (no more than ten lines).

2. One day you might be a parent. Will you want to help your children decide who to marry? Write down your ideas about this in a short letter to yourself to be opened at the age of 45.

## GETTING CLOSER – FOCUS ON DETAILS

### The start of the play

The Birlings, a well-to-do family, have gathered to celebrate the engagement of their daughter, Sheila, to Gerald Croft. They sit around a large dining table in the centre of the stage. We can tell by the **setting** and the costumes that this is just before the First World War. We find out shortly that the year is 1912.

1. Read the opening stage directions. Then copy the following table and use it to list the details Priestley gives and to explain what these details reveal about each character.

| Character | Details | What the details reveal |
|---|---|---|
| Arthur Birling | 'in evening dress', 'white tie', 'heavy-looking', 'portentous', 'provincial in his speech' | wealthy and well-dressed<br>a bit pompous-looking – wanting to impress?<br>speech that can be rural in origin – maybe not as sophisticated-sounding as Birling would like? |
| Sybil Birling | | |
| Eric Birling | | |
| Sheila Birling | | |
| Gerald Croft | | |
| Edna | | |

2. How do you think Priestley wants his audience to feel about the Birling family at the opening of the play? Discuss this in small groups.

### First impressions of Sheila

In this section, you will explore the character of Sheila and the relationships between different characters in the play. During these activities, you should use references from the text to support the points you make. Keep your quotations short and to the point. Identify key words that you could use in your writing.

1. Look closely at Sheila's lines in the first section of the play, before the arrival of the Inspector.

   a  What are your first impressions of Sheila? Create a spider diagram to record your thoughts.
   
   b  Use the information from your spider diagram to write two or three paragraphs about your first impressions of Sheila's character. Write about **what she says** or **what others say about her** and use quotations from the text to support your opinion.

2. Choose two pairs of characters. In pairs, talk about what you think their attitudes are to each other at the start of the play. Remember to back up your opinions with evidence from the text.

3. Choose any three characters. Write a paragraph for each character, explaining what they think of the others. Write in the **first person**, as if you are the character. Try to make sure that your ideas and opinions are true to the text.

**Key terms**

**setting:** the description of the place in which a story is set.

**first person:** a way of writing that tells a story through the eyes of one of the characters, using the pronouns 'I', 'my' and 'me'.

*All five are in evening dress of the period, the men in tails and white ties.*

Stage direction: Act One

# GCSE English Literature for AQA: An Inspector Calls

## PUTTING DETAILS TO USE

### Characters and relationships

We've selected this extract to help you develop your understanding of the play and so that you can have more confidence to use textual evidence in your written responses.

**Eric** (*rather noisily*) All the best! She's got a nasty temper sometimes – but she's not bad really. Good old Sheila!

**Sheila** Chump! I can't drink to this, can I? When do I drink?

**Gerald** You can drink to me.

**Sheila** (*quiet and serious now*) All right then. I drink to you, Gerald.

*For a moment they look at each other.*

**Gerald** (*quietly*) Thank you. And I drink to you – and hope I can make you as happy as you deserve to be.

**Sheila** (*trying to be light and easy*) You be careful – or I'll start weeping.

**Gerald** (*smiling*) Well, perhaps this will help to stop it. (*He produces a ring case.*)

**Sheila** (*excited*) Oh – Gerald – you've got it – is it the one you wanted me to have?

**Gerald** (*giving the case to her*) Yes – the very one.

**Sheila** (*taking out the ring*) Oh – it's wonderful! Look – Mummy – isn't it a beauty? Oh – darling – (*She kisses* GERALD *hastily.*)

**Eric** Steady the Buffs!

**Sheila** (*who has put ring on, admiringly*) I think it's perfect. Now I really feel engaged.

**Mrs B.** So you ought, darling. It's a lovely ring. Be careful with it.

**Sheila** Careful! I'll never let it go out of my sight for an instant.

**Mrs B.** (*smiling*) Well, it came just at the right moment. That was clever of you, Gerald. Now, Arthur, if you've no more to say, I think Sheila and I had better go into the drawing-room and leave you men—

**Birling** (*rather heavily*) I just want to say this. (*Noticing that* SHEILA *is still admiring her ring.*) Are you listening, Sheila? This concerns you too. And after all I don't often make speeches at you—

**Sheila** I'm sorry, Daddy. Actually I was listening.

*She looks attentive, as they all do. He holds them for a moment before continuing.*

# 1 Home sweet home

**1** Working in groups of four, take part in a 'silent discussion' about Sheila:

- Place a large sheet of paper in the middle of a table and write 'Sheila's character' in the middle.
- You have eight minutes to write notes, ideas and sketches about Sheila's character at this point in the play.
- You can communicate with each other as much as you like, but **only** through writing. You must not talk to each other.

You may have to work out some things about her character by what she says and by what other characters say about her. For example Eric says: '**She's got a nasty temper**'. This might imply that she is rather spoilt and that she bosses her brother around.

Use the notes you make in this activity to help you with the writing task at the end of the unit.

**2** Now you are going to put Sheila in the hot-seat. Each person in the group should write down four questions that they would like to ask Sheila, then follow the steps below. Try to make your questions open and challenging. For example:

- Why do you think your brother Eric says you have a nasty temper?
- Why do you go quiet when Gerald asks you to drink to him?

a  Place one chair with three others facing it.
b  Take it in turns to sit in the hot-seat, in role as Sheila.
c  Answer the questions put to you by the other three in the group. They should make notes of your answers.
d  If you don't know the answer to a question, make something up!

 Watch some actors preparing questions for Sheila on Cambridge Elevate.

 **Learning checkpoint**

Use your four questions from the hot-seat activity to write a short 'question-and-answer' interview with Sheila. You could write this as an article for a magazine. In your interview or article, you should:

✔ show what you know and understand about Sheila's character and use some quoted details from the text
✔ include your own interpretation of the character of Sheila.

I think it's perfect. Now I really feel engaged.

*Sheila: Act One*

## Characterisation

When looking at people in a play or a novel, you need to be aware of the difference between **character** and **characterisation**.

If you watch a performance of *An Inspector Calls* and the actor playing Sheila is doing a good job, you will feel that Sheila is a real person. This is character. Characterisation is the methods that a writer uses to present a character to the audience and make them realistic.

 **Watch an actor discuss playing Sheila on Cambridge Elevate.**

Now that you have explored how Priestley presents Sheila's character to an audience, you are going to organise that information and plan a further piece of writing. Before you start, read through the extract again.

The following tasks and questions will help you understand Sheila's relationship with the other characters. Work in pairs to discuss or carry out each activity, making notes as you go.

1. How does Priestley use language in the extract to show the audience that Sheila is wealthy, attractive and intelligent?

2. Write down three quotations that suggest Sheila's life might be rather restricted.

3. Think about Sheila's relationship with her brother, Eric. Write a short paragraph summing up what Eric thinks about his sister. Include quotations from the text to support your interpretation.

4. Priestley writes the stage direction '**For a moment they look at each other**'. What do you think this detail means?

5. Write three bullet points to explain what the dramatic device of the ring tells us about the relationship between Gerald and Sheila.

6. What do you think Sheila's reaction to the ring suggests about the kind of young woman she is?

7. Sheila desribes the ring as '**perfect**'. What does the language Sheila uses tell us about her character at this point in the play?

8. Write a short paragraph about Sheila's relationship with her father. Support your opinions with at least one quotation from the text.

 **Read more about character and characterisation in the play in Unit 13.**

 **Key terms**

**character:** a person in a story; even when based on real people, characters in plays or novels are invented or fictionalised.
**characterisation:** the techniques a writer uses to describe characters and make them seem real.

## GETTING IT INTO WRITING

### Writing about the beginning of *An Inspector Calls*

You need to develop ways of showing your skills in your written responses to *An Inspector Calls*. Your writing for GCSE English Literature will be assessed on:

- your use of detail
- your own interpretations
- your understanding of Priestley's writing skill and techniques for the theatre
- your use of relevant terminology.

In your response to a question, you should:

- use detail from the text to support your interpretation
- consider how Priestley has created the characters
- show how Priestley's writing affects an audience
- interpret and analyse the text in a persuasive way.

The following three example student responses show how a basic answer can be improved.

**A basic answer** shows that you are familiar with what the characters **say** and **do**, and can make some comments on them:

*Mr Birling thinks he is very important. He keeps telling the others that he is a 'hard-headed' businessman and has been 'on the Bench' and a 'Mayor', and has a chance of becoming Sir Birling.*

**A good answer** shows that you can use quotations to explain **why** they are interesting or **why** they matter:

*Mr Birling is shown to be someone who likes people to know that he is successful and has held some high-status positions. This is because he is 'provincial' and his wife is his 'social superior', so he needs to draw attention to his achievements.*

**The best answers** show that you understand **how** characters have been created by a playwright. You explain what the characters say and do, and refer to the author's **ideas** and **purposes**:

Priestley makes Birling an arrogant, self-made man who is anxious to get on with upper-class people like the Crofts and to raise his social status. Priestley does this by his use of stage directions to the actor and by writing speech that is full of self-praise and showing off. For example when Birling talks to Gerald, Priestley writes: 'Thanks. (*Confidentially.*) By the way, there's something I'd like to mention – in the strictest confidence – while we're by ourselves.' The playwright is showing us that Birling is very pleased that he can speak to a member of the aristocracy in such an equal way. He believes he has moved up in the world.

**1** Look back over your work so far. Aim to write two paragraphs in which you explain how Priestley introduces some of the characters and the relationships between them at the beginning of the play.

As you plan and write, make sure you:

- **a** consider the techniques Priestley uses to create his characters
- **b** back up your ideas with evidence from the text, using relevant quotations
- **c** use a range of vocabulary and sentence structures.

### Learning checkpoint

When you have finished, swap your response with a partner and read each other's work. Assess each other on how well you have:

- ✔ commented on relevant selected textual detail
- ✔ made some personal interpretation of characters and relationships
- ✔ explored the playwright's ideas and attitudes
- ✔ used a range of vocabulary and sentence structures
- ✔ used accurate spelling and punctuation.

**Complete this assignment on Cambridge Elevate.**

# 1 Home sweet home

## GETTING FURTHER

### Turning points

In this unit, you have focused on Sheila's character at the beginning of her journey.

 As you read and watch the play, make a note of the major **turning points** for her character. Try to find two or three extracts that are significant points in Sheila's journey.

 Use the same technique to explore the journeys of the characters of Gerald, Eric and Birling.

### Sketching Sheila

1. Spend no more than five minutes doing a pencil sketch of Sheila, paying particular attention to the costume she might wear.

   a  Draw an expression on her face that sums up her attitude in the extract in this unit.
   b  Add some labels and annotations to your drawing to explain the choices for your design.

2. Work in pairs. **A** is the director of the play, **B** is the designer. **B** has to pitch a design for Sheila's costume to **A**.

   **A** As the director of the play, you will want to interrogate every aspect of the designer's ideas. Have they properly understood the character?
   **B** Remember, as the designer you will be keen to explain how the detail of your design expresses Sheila's character.

> Hear more about the designer's job on Cambridge Elevate.

> **Key terms**
>
> **turning points:** in any drama, characters have important moments in which their character changes or develops; these key moments are referred to as 'turning points'.

> Well, don't do any. We'll drink their health and have done with it.
>
> *Eric: Act One*

# 2

## Confidence and conflict

How does Priestley create dramatic impact in his presentation of the Inspector?

Your progress in this unit:
- explore how Priestley makes the arrival of the Inspector dramatically interesting
- understand and explain the way Priestley uses stagecraft
- explore the way he uses theatricality and dramatic devices
- interpret the way he moves the text into performance
- develop a response to writing tasks.

## GETTING STARTED – THE PLAY AND YOU

### A life of luxury

*An Inspector Calls* is set in 1912. The **setting** and situation of the play suggest that the Birlings are wealthy and lead a comfortable life.

**1** Discuss the following questions in pairs or small groups.

  a  What do you think life would have been like for a wealthy family at this time?
  b  In what ways would their lives have been different to those of poor people (the type of people who worked in the factories that the Birlings owned)?
  c  What kind of people do you think families like the Birlings would have been? Why? Explain your answers.

## GETTING CLOSER – FOCUS ON DETAILS

### Key moments

Read the play from the end of the extract in Unit 1 to the point where the Inspector explains the reason for his visit.

**1** In most scenes of a play there is a key moment – the point at which the action takes off. Which of the following quotations from this section represents the key moment in this scene? Explain your choice to a partner.

  a  Edna: Please, sir, an inspector's called.
  b  Inspector: Two hours ago a young woman died in the Infirmary. She'd been taken there this afternoon because she'd swallowed a lot of strong disinfectant. Burnt her inside out, of course.
  c  Gerald: (*lightly*) Sure to be. Unless Eric's been up to something. (*Nodding confidentially to* BIRLING.) And that would be awkward, wouldn't it?
  d  Birling: Well, what can I do for you? Some trouble about a warrant?

2 Confidence and conflict

## WHAT HAPPENS NEXT?

Just after Gerald gives Sheila the engagement ring, Birling makes a speech to the family. He says that they are marrying at a good time because employers are coming together in the interests of capital.

He is scornful of the idea that there will be war and illustrates his optimism by referring to the 'unsinkable' *Titanic*.

Sheila and Mrs Birling leave the room. Birling confides to Gerald that he is hopeful of receiving a knighthood. Above all, he tells Eric and Gerald: '**a man has to mind his own business and look after himself and his own**'.

At this moment, the doorbell rings and Edna introduces the Inspector. The Inspector explains he would like some information because a young woman has just died after swallowing strong disinfectant.

### Establishing Mr Birling's character

The **character** of Birling is very arrogant and self-assured, but an audience knows that much of Birling's confidence about the future is misplaced.

**1** Copy and complete the following table to show how Birling is wrong about the future.

| Birling's confidence | What the audience knows and thinks |
| --- | --- |
| He is scornful of the idea that there will be a war. | The First World War will break out in two years time, in 1914. |
| He knows the miners have come out on strike but he says this is nothing to worry about. | |
| He explains that the *Titanic* is unsinkable and he sees it as a symbol of the power of capital. | |
| He says there will be peace, prosperity and rapid progress everywhere. | |
| He thinks he will be given a knighthood. | |
| He believes that a man is an individual who has to look after himself. | |

**2** The audience knows that many things Birling believes about the future will prove to be wrong. What effect does that have on how we feel about him? Discuss your ideas in pairs.

 Read more about character and characterisation in the play in Unit 13.

**3** Using the information in your completed table, write a paragraph describing the character of Birling as he is presented in the first scene. Use short quotations to support your points.

25

# GCSE English Literature for AQA: An Inspector Calls

## PUTTING DETAILS TO USE

### Plot and theatricality

We've selected this extract to help you develop your understanding of the play and so that you can have more confidence to use textual evidence in your written responses.

---

                    EDNA *enters.*

**Edna**      Please, sir, an inspector's called.

**Birling**   An inspector? What kind of inspector?

**Edna**      A police inspector. He says his name's Inspector Goole.

**Birling**   Don't know him. Does he want to see me?

**Edna**      Yes, sir. He says it's important.

**Birling**   All right, Edna. Show him in here. Give us some more light.

                    EDNA *does, then goes out.*

              I'm still on the Bench. It may be something about a warrant.

**Gerald**    (*lightly*) Sure to be. Unless Eric's been up to something. (*Nodding confidentially to* BIRLING.) And that would be awkward, wouldn't it?

**Birling**   (*humorously*) Very.

**Eric**      (*who is uneasy, sharply*) Here, what do you mean?

**Gerald**    (*lightly*) Only something we were talking about when you were out. A joke really.

**Eric**      (*still uneasy*) Well, I don't think it's very funny.

**Birling**   (*sharply, staring at him*) What's the matter with you?

**Eric**      (*defiantly*) Nothing.

**Edna**      (*opening door, and announcing*) Inspector Goole.

              *The* INSPECTOR *enters, and* EDNA *goes, closing door after her. The* INSPECTOR *need not be a big man but he creates at once an impression of massiveness, solidity and purposefulness. He is a man in his fifties, dressed in a plain darkish suit of the period. He speaks carefully, weightily, and has a disconcerting habit of looking hard at the person he addresses before actually speaking.*

**Inspector** Mr Birling?

**Birling**   Yes. Sit down, Inspector.

**Inspector** (*sitting*) Thank you, sir.

**Birling**   Have a glass of port – or a little whisky?

**Inspector** No, thank you, Mr Birling. I'm on duty.

**Birling**   You're new, aren't you?

2 Confidence and conflict

**Inspector** Yes, sir. Only recently transferred.

**Birling** I thought you must be. I was an alderman for years – and Lord Mayor two years ago – and I'm still on the Bench – so I know the Brumley police officers pretty well – and I thought I'd never seen you before.

**Inspector** Quite so.

**Birling** Well, what can I do for you? Some trouble about a warrant?

**Inspector** No, Mr Birling.

**Birling** (*after a pause, with a touch of impatience*) Well, what is it then?

**Inspector** I'd like some information, if you don't mind, Mr Birling. Two hours ago a young woman died in the Infirmary. She'd been taken there this afternoon because she'd swallowed a lot of strong disinfectant. Burnt her inside out, of course.

**Eric** (*involuntarily*) My God!

---

**1** The doorbell rings but the Inspector does not come on stage immediately. Instead, he is introduced by Edna. This makes his entrance dramatically interesting.

   **a** Work in pairs. Talk about what you think audience members imagine when they hear the word 'inspector'.
   **b** Create a spider diagram to record the notes from your discussion. Highlight five key words from your notes on your spider diagram.
   **c** Using your key words, write a paragraph about how you imagine the character of the Inspector before he appears on stage.

**2** Look again at the stage directions for the entrance of the Inspector. Identify all the words in this description that give the Inspector authority.

**3** When Edna announces the arrival of an inspector, Birling seems to think that Eric might be in trouble. What might the audience be thinking at this moment?

Read more about plot in Unit 11.

# A police inspector. He says his name's Inspector Goole.

*Edna: Act One*

## Character and language

Read the extract again, then answer the following questions.

1. What does Gerald's stage direction '*nodding confidently*' tell the audience about his relationship with Birling?

2. What evidence can you find in the text to suggest that Eric is uneasy when the Inspector arrives? Why do you think he feels like this?

3. Study the Inspector's language. Which of the following statements best explains the way he speaks? Find two quotations from the extract to support your answer.

   a   The Inspector is a big, powerful man and therefore he uses complex and sophisticated language.

   b   The Inspector makes short statements with no embellishment. He gives little away about himself and this gives him an air of both mystery and authority.

   c   The Inspector asks skilful questions so that he can interrogate the characters who he believes are suspects in a crime.

4. We know that Birling likes to impress people with his powerful position in society. Write a short paragraph examining how Birling tries to impress the Inspector when he arrives. Use at least one quotation to support your argument.

5. Choose any moment from the beginning of this section.

   a   Write the characters' names in a circle on a blank sheet of paper.

   b   Write brief notes to summarise each character's thoughts at this moment, and their attitude to the other characters. Use quotations and key words in your notes.

   c   Draw arrows to show the relationships between characters.

**Watch some actors create a freeze frame of this scene on Cambridge Elevate.**

## Dramatic devices

In this section, you will explore some of the dramatic devices Priestley uses and the terms used to describe them. It is useful to understand **why** the dramatist has used these devices and what effect they have. For example:

- Why does Priestley feel it necessary to write these stage directions at this point?
- What is Priestley trying to achieve by using dramatic tension in this scene?

Look at the list of dramatic devices:

> **protagonist:** the main character of the play or the scene.
> **climax:** the point in the play or scene where the drama reaches the greatest tension.
> **complication:** the point where the action of the scene becomes more intense.
> **conflict:** where two or more characters oppose each other.
> **exposition:** a detailed explanation of a situation or event.
> **falling action:** the action in the scene after the climax.
> **foreshadowing:** a hint at what will happen later in the play.
> **dramatic irony:** when the audience knows and understands something that a character does not.
> **pathos:** a quality of the play's action that makes an audience feel pity for a character.
> **dramatic tension:** the way in which suspense is developed in the scene. This is how the playwright keeps the audience interested.
> **inciting incident:** the point at which the action of the play or the scene really takes off.

**1** Copy the following table. Decide which dramatic device best fits each example and write it in the second column.

| Example | Dramatic device |
|---|---|
| Eric: (*involuntarily*) My God! | |
| *The* INSPECTOR | |
| EDNA *does, then goes out.* | |
| They did everything they could for her at the Infirmary, but she died. Suicide, of course. | |
| Birling: (*sharply, staring at him*) What's the matter with you? | |
| Eric: (*defiantly*) Nothing. | |
| Inspector: Two hours ago a young girl died in the Infirmary. | |
| Birling: I was an alderman for years – and Lord Mayor two years ago – and I'm still on the Bench. | |

### Learning checkpoint

Using the notes you have produced for the activities in this unit so far, write a paragraph about the effect created by the arrival of the Inspector in this section of the play. You should:

✔ consider how Priestley introduces the character of the Inspector
✔ give your own interpretation of the dramatic effect of the introduction of the Inspector
✔ show how his arrival affects what the other characters say and do
✔ use evidence from the text to support your points.

> I was an alderman for years – and Lord Mayor two years ago – and I'm still on the Bench.
>
> *Birling: Act One*

# GETTING IT INTO WRITING

## Prepare an essay plan

Now you are going to use the notes you have made to prepare an essay plan on how Priestley makes the arrival of the Inspector dramatically interesting.

You should include:

- evidence that you know and understand the text
- information on how Priestley uses language to show conflict between Birling and the Inspector
- Priestley's use of stage directions
- Priestley's use of dramatic techniques to create tension at this point in the play.

Use the following sample responses to the question to help you plan your own response.

A **basic answer** shows that you are familiar with what the characters **say** and **do**, and can make some comments on them:

*The arrival of the Inspector is announced by Edna, 'Please, sir, an inspector's called.'*

**A good answer** shows that you can use quotations to explain **why** they are interesting or important:

*The arrival of the Inspector is announced by Edna, 'Please, sir, an inspector's called.' Because we know the play is called An Inspector Calls we expect this will be a dramatic moment in the play. The word 'Inspector' reminds us of a crime drama and we suspect that someone in the room is in trouble.*

**The best answers** show that you understand **how** characters have been created by a playwright. You explain what the characters say and do and refer to the author's **ideas** and **purposes**:

*Priestley makes the arrival of the Inspector dramatically interesting by the announcement from Edna, 'Please, sir, an inspector's called.' Priestley uses our prior knowledge of crime drama by using the word 'inspector'. He allows us to visualise the Inspector by delaying his entrance. This creates suspense. We know something interesting is about to happen and we await the inciting incident with expectation.*

**1** Write your essay plan, following these steps:

  **a** Allow yourself six minutes.
  **b** Spend five minutes listing or making a spider diagram of all that you have discovered about how Priestley creates dramatic interest at this point in the play.
  **c** When you have finished your list or spider diagram, number everything according to what you are going to write about first, second, third and so on. Give yourself one minute to do this.

Focus your plan on details in the text using the following ideas:

- Before the arrival of the Inspector, Birling has been making a speech with great confidence.
- The arrival of the Inspector is announced by Edna.
- Birling tries to dominate the Inspector.
- The Inspector speaks in short, simple statements with an air of authority.
- The Inspector delays telling the characters about the death of the young woman.
- He describes her death in simple but vivid detail.

**2** When you have finished your plan, swap with a partner. Borrow three ideas from their plan and add them to your own.

 Complete this assignment on Cambridge Elevate.

 Watch a writer talking through ideas for this activity on Cambridge Elevate.

# 2 Confidence and conflict

### Learning checkpoint

Use your plan to write the first 300–500 words in response to the question. Make sure that you:

- ✔ comment on relevant details from the text, showing a clear response
- ✔ interpret characters and relationships, showing a developed response
- ✔ explore Priestley's ideas and purposes, with a convincing critical response
- ✔ use a range of vocabulary and sentence structures with accurate spelling and punctuation.

## GETTING FURTHER

### Stage action

**1** Read this section of the play again. Identify any clues about how the characters should move and act, and what should happen on stage. This might include things that the characters say, as well as the stage directions.

**2** Imagine you are the director of the play. Choose five lines from the section covered in this unit and write a commentary for them. Remember, the director will:

- be responsible for the overall vision of the production
- have lots of suggestions for how an actor should play their part
- have thought about the ideas in the scene.

Use the following example to help you:

| | |
|---|---|
| **Edna** | Please, sir, an inspector's called. |
| **Birling** | An inspector? What kind of inspector? |
| **Edna** | A police inspector. He says his name's Inspector Goole. |

Edna is a servant, so I would like her to stand to the side. I think there will be a little pause after her line because the audience will realise this is an important moment – after all, they know the play is called *An Inspector Calls*.

At this point Birling will need to be irritated. He's not really worried about anything and thinks it's to do with his job. I'll get him to be a bit offhand and rude to Edna in the tone he uses.

Perhaps she's being a bit cheeky here. Maybe Edna likes the idea that Birling could be in trouble.

# 3

## Rights and responsibilities

How does Priestley use Birling to explore the theme of social responsibility?

Your progress in this unit:
- explore how Priestley uses the Inspector and Birling to develop ideas about responsibility
- understand and analyse the social and political context of the play
- form an opinion about the play's relevance today
- develop a response to writing tasks.

## GETTING STARTED – THE PLAY AND YOU

In this unit you will think about how Priestley uses the Inspector, Birling and the action of this part of the play to explore the ideas of rights and responsibilities. You will find out about some of the political and social ideas that influenced Priestley when he was writing the play.

**1** In pairs, look at the following scenario:

The **setting** is a fast-food café.
**A** works as a waiter or waitress.
**B** owns the café.
**A** finds out that they are working for less than the minimum wage.
**A** goes to **B** and asks for a pay rise.

Act out the conversation.

**2** Afterwards, note down three bullet points for each side of the argument – for and against a pay rise. Which side do you agree with? Why? At the end of this unit, decide if your opinions have changed.

## GETTING CLOSER – FOCUS ON DETAILS

### Who thinks what?

Read the play from the end of the extract in Unit 2 up to the point where Birling explains why Eva Smith was dismissed from the factory.

**1** Look at the following table about each **character**'s attitude towards rights and responsibilities. The attitudes have been jumbled up. Match the correct attitude to the appropriate character.

| Character | Attitude to rights and responsibilities |
|---|---|
| Inspector | Thinks it would be impossible to be responsible for everything we do. |
| Birling | Believes that workers have the right to be paid a fair wage and people have a responsibility to speak up for others. |
| Eva Smith | Believes that events are linked together and that this might make us responsible in a way we had not realised. |
| Eric | Believes they have nothing to do with this and should not be present. |
| Gerald | Is interested by what the Inspector says and seems to want to know more. |

## WHAT HAPPENS NEXT?

The Inspector explains that the girl's death was suicide, and that her name was Eva Smith, although she used a number of different names.

He says that she left a sort of diary and he shows her photograph to Birling, refusing to let Eric or Gerald see it.

Birling clearly recognises her as a past employee. He explains that he discharged her because she was the ringleader of a group of workers who were asking for more money.

Birling says he has a duty to keep labour costs down and he doesn't see that it has anything to do with **'the wretched girl's suicide'**.

# GCSE English Literature for AQA: An Inspector Calls

## PUTTING DETAILS TO USE

### The theme of social responsibility

*An Inspector Calls* was written in 1945. This was right at the end of the Second World War, during which people from different social classes had fought alongside each other. People were beginning to think about their responsibilities towards each other and Priestley wanted to explore this theme in his play.

We've selected this extract to help you develop your understanding of the play and so that you can have more confidence to use textual evidence in your written responses.

---

**Inspector** Because what happened to her then may have determined what happened to her afterwards, and what happened to her afterwards may have driven her to suicide. A chain of events.

**Birling** Oh well – put like that, there's something in what you say. Still, I can't accept any responsibility. If we were all responsible for everything that happened to everybody we'd had anything to do with, it would be very awkward, wouldn't it?

**Inspector** Very awkward.

**Birling** We'd all be in an impossible position, wouldn't we?

**Eric** By Jove, yes. And as you were saying, Dad, a man has to look after himself—

**Birling** Yes, well, we needn't go into all that.

**Inspector** Go into what?

**Birling** Oh – just before you came – I'd been giving these young men a little good advice. Now – about this girl, Eva Smith. I remember her quite well now. She was a lively good-looking girl – country-bred, I fancy – and she'd been working in one of our machine shops for over a year. A good worker too. In fact, the foreman there told me he was ready to promote her into what we call a leading operator – head of a small group of girls. But after they came back from their holidays that August, they were all rather restless, and they suddenly decided to ask for more money. They were averaging about twenty-two and six, which was neither more nor less than is paid generally in our industry. They wanted the rates raised so that they could average about twenty-five shillings a week. I refused, of course.

**Inspector** Why?

**Birling** (*surprised*) Did you say 'Why?'?

**Inspector** Yes. Why did you refuse?

**Birling** Well, Inspector, I don't see that it's any concern of yours how I choose to run my business. Is it now?

**Inspector** It might be, you know.

**Birling** I don't like that tone.

**Inspector** I'm sorry. But you asked me a question.

**Birling** And you asked me a question before that, a quite unnecessary question too.

**Inspector** It's my duty to ask questions.

**Birling** Well, it's my duty to keep labour costs down, and if I'd agreed to this demand for a new rate we'd have added about twelve per cent to our labour costs. Does that satisfy you? So I refused. Said I couldn't consider it. We were paying the usual rates and if they didn't like those rates, they could go and work somewhere else. It's a free country, I told them.

**Eric** It isn't if you can't go and work somewhere else.

**Inspector** Quite so.

---

1. What do Birling's words '**restless**' and '**suddenly decided**' reveal about his attitude to the workers? Discuss this in pairs.

2. Look again at Birling's description of how the workers in his factory asked for higher pay. Write two paragraphs to explain what the language in this speech reveals about Birling's attitude towards his workers.

3. Think about what you have learnt from this extract about Birling's views on running the factory. Create a spider diagram with the words 'Birling's views on running the factory' in the centre. Add notes to the diagram, using quotations from the text.

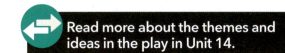

Read more about the themes and ideas in the play in Unit 14.

4. The Inspector talks about a '**chain of events**'. What do you think he means? How does this link to the theme of social responsibility?

# Well, Inspector, I don't see that it's any concern of yours how I choose to run my business. Is it now?

*Birling: Act One*

## Character and language

**1** Look again at Birling's description of how the workers came to him, asking for more money. Write out this event in the form of a short play script. Try to use language typical of the characters.

**2** Eric says, '**It isn't if you can't go and work somewhere else.**' What does this suggest about his relationship with his father?

**3** Towards the end of this section, Birling becomes increasingly irritated with the Inspector. They have an exchange of short, sharp lines. Why do you think Birling behaves like this? Rank the following statements in order, with the most relevant at the top.

    **a** Birling feels that the Inspector is getting the better of him.
    **b** He feels guilty about dismissing Eva Smith.
    **c** He realises that the Inspector has a different attitude to his own.
    **d** He wants the Inspector to go away so that he can get back to enjoying the evening with his family.

**4** What reasons does Birling give for not agreeing to the pay rise? He says it is his '**duty to keep labour costs down**'. Why do you think this is important to him?

### Learning checkpoint

Either make notes or annotate a copy of the extract to show evidence of Priestley's attitude about social responsibility. For example Birling says:

If we were all responsible for everything that happened to everybody we'd had anything to do with, it would be very awkward, wouldn't it?

Birling clearly has the opposite view to Priestley: he does not believe in the importance of society or being responsible for one another.

## GETTING IT INTO WRITING

### Writing about the theme of social responsibility

In this unit, you have seen how Priestley explores the idea of social responsibility through his characters. You will now have the opportunity to use your notes from this unit to produce a short written response.

**1** Write about how Priestly explores responsibility in the extract you have read in this unit. You should aim to write about 300 words in your answer.

You should include:

a  evidence that you know and understand about Birling's attitudes – his perspective on the events that led to Eva being dismissed
b  evidence from the text to show how the other characters represent attitudes of people at the time the play is set
c  some of your own interpretation about Priestley's presentation of ideas – through what the characters say and in the stage directions.

**2** When you have finished, swap your work with a partner and read their response. Assess their answer using the three prompts as a guide.

**3** Compare your answers. Discuss the similarities and differences, then select:

a  three ideas in your answer that you can suggest to your partner
b  three ideas of theirs that you can copy or learn from.

**Complete this assignment on Cambridge Elevate.**

### Learning checkpoint

**How will I know I've done this well?**
- ✔ **The best answers** will show that you understand how Priestley presents his characters. For example you will write about what Birling says and does but you will also comment on how Priestley shows Birling to be self-centred and out of step with what is happening.
- ✔ **Good answers** will show a clear understanding of the characters and what ideas they represent. Comments about Birling will be backed up with well-chosen quotations. You will comment on specific words or phrases used in the text. You will use accurate spelling and clear, well-punctuated sentences.
- ✔ **Weaker answers** will comment on the characters in general, using few or no specific examples and without mentioning how Priestley uses them to comment on the theme of social responsibility.

## GETTING FURTHER

### Create a two-minute documentary

You are going to create a short **documentary** about Priestley's life and the **context** of the times in which he was writing.

Here are some points about Priestley and *An Inspector Calls* to help you write the voiceover for your documentary. You will have to decide which to use and how to arrange them.

> **Facts**
> - People in the audience would have survived the Second World War and possibly the First World War.
> - In 1945, the Labour Party came to power.
> - Priestley was born in Yorkshire in 1894.
> - At the age of 16, he got a job as a clerk for a wool firm.
> - Priestley fought in the First World War.
> - He wrote many novels and plays that were considered controversial.
> - He wrote about new ideas with strong political messages.
> - He set up a new political party that fought for public ownership of land and greater democracy in Britain. This party merged with the Labour Party.
> - His wartime radio programme was attacked by the Conservatives and cancelled by the BBC for being too left-wing.
> - He supported the idea of the Welfare State – the belief that the state and society have a duty to care for all its citizens.
> - He believed that further wars could only be avoided by co-operation between countries.
> - Women were seen as having made a vital contribution to the war effort in both world wars.
> - Priestley chose to set his play in 1912 – a time very different from the one in which he was writing.
> - He explores ideas about socialism and capitalism.
> - He uses the play to encourage people to build a better and more caring society.

**1** Use the fact file to write the voiceover for a two-minute documentary about the background to *An Inspector Calls*. The information is not in any particular order so you will need to choose which pieces of information to use and what order to present them in. You will also need to rewrite the notes to make them more interesting for your audience.

**2** When you are happy with the draft of your voiceover, use a copy of the following template to create a **storyboard** for your documentary. Find appropriate still images, music or quotations to illustrate what is being said. Some examples have been given, but you can use your own ideas.

| Visual | Voiceover | Music and sound effects |
|---|---|---|
| | | Music – 'My Dreams are Getting Better All the Time' by Les Brown |
| (photograph of woman and man with pram) | When the audience sat down to watch *An Inspector Calls* in 1945, the Second World War had changed the world that people lived in. | |
| | Many homes had been bombed and people were having to build new lives. | An air-raid siren |
| (photograph of soldier with gun) | | 'I came back from fighting in Burma. I expected to be a hero but everyone had forgotten about us. Toffs and such looking down on you and I said to myself, "things have got to change".' |

 **3** When you have finished your storyboard, compare it with others in your class. If you have access to editing facilities, film and edit your two-minute documentary.

> **Key terms**
>
> **documentary:** a film that uses pictures or interviews with people involved in real events to provide a report on a subject; documentaries can contain opinion, but they should be based on facts and evidence.
> **context:** the historical circumstances of a piece of writing, which affect what an author wrote and the way they wrote it.
> **storyboard:** a sequence of drawings that show the different scenes in a story.

# 4

## Complaints and consequences

How does Priestley present Sheila's changing attitudes?

Your progress in this unit:
- examine the changing attitudes of Sheila and how the other characters influence these
- explore how form and structure influence the choices the playwright makes
- produce a piece of creative writing that moves from a play script to a screenplay
- develop a response to writing tasks.

## GETTING STARTED – THE PLAY AND YOU

Read the play from the end of the extract in Unit 3 to where Sheila describes what happened in the clothes shop.

**1** What would you have done if you were the manager at Milwards and were faced with Sheila's complaint? Would you have dismissed Eva Smith? Discuss this in groups, giving reasons for your answers.

**2** Is the customer always right? Have you or your friends been faced with a similar situation when someone complained about you, or have you ever complained about the service in a shop or other place?

## GETTING CLOSER – FOCUS ON DETAILS

### The world beyond the stage

Read the summary of what happens in this section. Then read the extract that follows and answer the questions. They will help you focus on some of the details Priestley uses to illustrate the world of the characters. Make notes of your answers. You can use these later when you come to plan your own answer to an essay question.

**1** Priestley writes the stage direction, '*Enter* SHEILA, *who looks as if she's been crying.*' This suggests there is a world outside the room where other events are happening at the same time. What other examples can you find of reference to the world outside in the play so far?

**2** Sheila closes the door as she comes into the room. What might this suggest about the decisions she has made outside?

**3** Sheila says, '**I'd persuade mother to close our account with them**'. Write a paragraph that explains what this reveals about the shop's relationship with the Birlings.

**4** Look at the exchange between Sheila and Gerald. Who do you think has the power in the relationship? Why do you think this?

**5** Sheila asks, '**So I'm really responsible?**' Write a paragraph that explains why you think these words might be significant in the play.

4 Complaints and consequences

## WHAT HAPPENS NEXT?

The Inspector explains that Eva Smith took a job working at Milwards, a clothes shop. She liked working there but was told she would '**have to go**' after a customer complained about her.

Sheila becomes uncomfortable and asks what the girl looked like. The Inspector shows her a photo. Sheila '*recognizes it with a little cry, gives a stifled sob, and then runs out.*'

After some moments she comes back in. Sheila says that she was responsible for the girl's dismissal. She tells the story of a dress she wanted to try on. It did not suit her, but when it was held up to the shop assistant it was just right for her. Sheila was jealous and told the manager that the girl had been impertinent.

41

*Enter* SHEILA, *who looks as if she's been crying.*

**Inspector** Well, Miss Birling?

**Sheila** (*coming in, closing door*): You knew it was me all the time, didn't you?

**Inspector** I had an idea it might be – from something the girl herself wrote.

**Sheila** I've told my father – he didn't seem to think it amounted to much – but I felt rotten about it at the time and now I feel a lot worse. Did it make much difference to her?

**Inspector** Yes, I'm afraid it did. It was the last real steady job she had. When she lost it – for no reason that she could discover – she decided she might as well try another kind of life.

**Sheila** (*miserably*) So I'm really responsible?

**Inspector** No, not entirely. A good deal happened to her after that. But you're partly to blame. Just as your father is.

**Eric** But what did Sheila do?

**Sheila** (*distressed*) I went to the manager at Milwards and I told him that if they didn't get rid of that girl, I'd never go near the place again and I'd persuade mother to close our account with them.

**Inspector** And why did you do that?

**Sheila** Because I was in a furious temper.

**Inspector** And what had this girl done to make you lose your temper?

**Sheila** When I was looking at myself in the mirror I caught sight of her smiling at the assistant, and I was furious with her. I'd been in a bad temper anyhow.

**Inspector** And was it the girl's fault?

**Sheila** No, not really. It was my own fault. (*Suddenly, to* GERALD) All right, Gerald, you needn't look at me like that. At least, I'm trying to tell the truth. I expect you've done things you're ashamed of too.

**Gerald** (*surprised*) Well, I never said I hadn't. I don't see why—

**Inspector** (*cutting in*) Never mind about that. You can settle that between you afterwards. (*To* SHEILA.) What happened?

**Sheila** I'd gone in to try something on. It was an idea of my own – mother had been against it, and so had the assistant – but I insisted. As soon as I tried it on, I knew they'd been right. It just didn't suit me at all. I looked silly in the thing. Well, this girl had brought the dress up from the workroom, and when the assistant – Miss Francis – had asked her something about it, this girl, to show us what she meant, had held the dress up, as if she was wearing it. And it just suited her. She was the right type for it, just as I was the wrong type. She was a very pretty girl too – with big dark eyes – and that didn't make it any better. Well, when I tried the thing on and looked at myself and knew that it was all wrong, I caught sight of this girl smiling at Miss Francis – as if to say: 'Doesn't she look awful' – and I was absolutely furious. I was very rude to both of them, and then I went to the manager and told him that this girl had been very impertinent – and – and – (*She almost breaks down, but just controls herself.*) How could I know what would happen afterwards? If she'd been some miserable plain little creature, I don't suppose I'd have done it. But she was very pretty and looked as if she could take care of herself.

## PUTTING DETAILS TO USE

### Characters and perspectives

These questions will help you focus on Sheila and how Priestley changes her ideas and attitudes as the play progresses. They will also help you think about the themes of responsibility, gender  and social class.

1. At the beginning of the extract, Sheila realises that the Inspector knows far more than he is letting on. What does this tell us about the way her character is developing?

2. Sheila says:

   I've told my father – he didn't seem to think it amounted to much – but I felt rotten about it at the time and now I feel a lot worse.

Write the conversation between Sheila and her father that happens off stage. Make sure you use your knowledge of the text, the characters and their actions to help you.

> **Key terms**
>
> **stereotype:** an oversimplified but common image or idea of a particular person or thing.

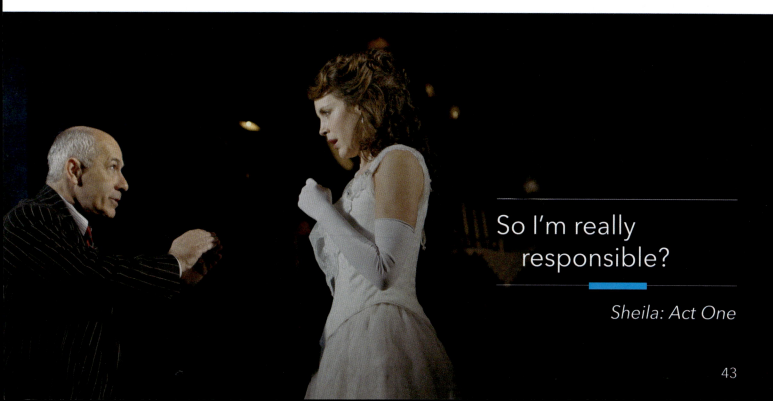

> So I'm really responsible?
>
> *Sheila: Act One*

3. Sheila is ashamed of her actions at Milwards. Find three examples of the language she uses that illustrate this. For example:

She was the right type for it, just as I was the wrong type.

4. Write a paragraph that explains how Sheila's attitudes are changing. Use these three phrases in your paragraph:

   a  Even before she comes into the room, Sheila has been thinking about … .
   b  Sheila uses language such as … , which helps show her guilt.
   c  By the end of the story, Sheila has … . However, she still says, 'How could I know what would happen afterwards?', which suggests that she is still trying to make an excuse for her actions.

## Themes – who is to blame

1. Summarise in bullet points how the following **characters** might be responsible for the death of Eva Smith:

   a  Birling
   b  Sheila.

2. In many ways, Sheila is typical of a young, upper middle-class woman of the time. Make a list of ways that she conforms to gender stereotype. For example:

   She is pretty.
   She spends her time shopping.

Find out more about themes and ideas in the play in Unit 14.

She was the right type for it, just as I was the wrong type.

*Sheila: Act One*

## 4 Complaints and consequences

### Learning checkpoint

Write a paragraph that explains how Sheila's actions at Milwards might be linked to the Inspector's ideas of a '**chain of events**'. Use at least one quotation from the text as evidence to support your comments.

**How will I know I've done this well?**

✔ comment on specific words or phrases used in the text
✔ explain something about Sheila's responsibility
✔ include some details about how Priestley develops Sheila's character
✔ use accurate spelling and clear, well-punctuated sentences.

## GETTING IT INTO WRITING

### Exploring Sheila's character

**1** Work on your own or in pairs. Create a spider diagram to summarise everything you know about Sheila's character up to this point in the play. Consider the following points to get you started:

  a  Her parents are wealthy.
  b  She does not work.
  c  She will be married to Gerald and her father is very keen on this marriage.

**2** Imagine that Sheila keeps a diary. Write a diary entry for a typical day in which she has taken a trip to town and visited some exclusive clothes shops. Remember to:

  a  use language, **setting** and ideas that are appropriate to 1912
  b  make sure that her diary reflects the ideas and attitudes that you have seen in her character so far in the play.

**3** Compare your diary entry with those of other students. Did you include similar details?

**4** In small groups, discuss how Priestley **characterises** Sheila at this point in the play. As the play progresses, you will see that as her character develops her ideas and attitudes change. The Inspector's questioning eventually makes her examine her own actions and their consequences.

**Complete this assignment on Cambridge Elevate.**

45

# GCSE English Literature for AQA: An Inspector Calls

## GETTING FURTHER

### Adapt an episode

You are going to produce an **adaptation** of the episode of Sheila's visit to Milwards, rewriting it as a **screenplay**. Remember, screenwriters have a saying that guides their writing: 'Show, don't tell.' In a play on the stage, like *An Inspector Calls*, we are happy to listen to a character **telling** us the story of events that have happened. In a film, however, we like to **see** events, not simply be told about them.

**1** First, plan your screenplay by following these steps:

   **a** Re-read Sheila's description of her visit to Milwards in the extract in this unit.
   **b** Write two lines that describe the shop. This is called the setting.
   **c** Make a list of the characters that Sheila mentions, so that you know how many characters are in your screenplay. Do you need to invent any that are not in the play?
   **d** Look closely at Sheila's story and, on a copy of the extract, underline any important **dialogue** that you might use in your screenplay.
   **e** Underline any key movements that are important in the scene.
   **f** Will you have to invent anything that is not in the play?

**2** Look closely at the following example of a short screenplay for an earlier part of the play. Pay particular attention to the way this is presented. Look, for example, at how character names are in the centre of the page (as in professional screenplays). Now use your notes and the screenplay template to write a draft of your scene. Aim to fill about two sides of A4.

---

```
              INT. DINING ROOM - NIGHT
Gerald looks at Sheila for a beat. He produces a neat and expensive ring case.
                       SHEILA
         Oh Gerald, you've got it. Is it the one you wanted me to have?
                       GERALD
         Yes - the very one.
He gives her the case. And she takes out a diamond ring.
                       SHEILA
         Oh it's wonderful! Look Mummy, isn't it a beauty?
She kisses Gerald.
         I think it's perfect. Now I feel really engaged.
Mrs Birling holds Sheila's hand as she studies the ring.
                       MRS BIRLING
         So you ought, darling. It's a lovely ring. Be careful with it.
```

**3** When you have finished the draft for your screenplay, swap your work with a partner.

   **a** Discuss the different choices that you have both made.
   **b** What have you decided to put in and what have you left out?

**4** You have now recreated this scene in a different form.

   **a** How has this affected the way in which the story has been told?
   **b** What changes have you made to the structure?

## Create a screenplay in a lesson

**1** Divide the play up amongst the class, so that each person takes two or three pages. Using the skills you have learnt in this unit, adapt your section of the play into a screenplay for a film.

When you have finished your individual section of screenplay, gather together all the sections that have been written by the class and put them in order to make a full screenplay for a new film adaptation of *An Inspector Calls*.

**2** An alternative is to take just two or three pages and adapt them in prose as an extract from a novel. Each form has its own strengths and weaknesses.

   **a** What are the advantages and disadvantages of writing in the form of a novel compared to a stage play or a screenplay?
   **b** Why do you think Priestley chose to write *An Inspector Calls* as a play for the stage?

### Key terms

**adaptation:** a text that has been changed from one form to another – for example from a play into a film.
**screenplay:** a script for a film.
**dialogue:** a conversation between two or more characters in a novel, play or film.

# 5 Truth and lies

How does Priestley use the Inspector to explore the theme of responsibility?

Your progress in this unit:
- understand and explore how Priestley uses the unique character of the Inspector
- illustrate and interrogate how Priestley characterises the Inspector
- explore the way Priestley presents characters to an audience
- work with a partner to produce a formal piece of writing about the Inspector.

## GETTING STARTED - THE PLAY AND YOU

### Getting to the truth

**1** The Inspector questions Sheila in a tough and quite brutal way. In pairs, discuss the following questions. Give reasons for your answers.

　a　Are such techniques justified when searching for the truth?

　b　Does it matter if the person is innocent? What if you are wrong and the person you question so harshly is completely innocent?

**2** Imagine that a student has discovered something of theirs has been stolen from the classroom. Is it acceptable for the teacher to keep the whole class in at break time for questioning? Why, or why not?

**3** Do you think the Inspector is justified in accusing Sheila of playing a part in Eva's death?

## GETTING CLOSER - FOCUS ON DETAILS

### The action so far

Read the play from the end of the extract in Unit 4 to the end of Act One.

**1** Look at the following quotations from the play so far. Put them in order without looking back at the text. When you have finished, scan the text to see if your order is correct.

　a　Inspector: Two hours ago a young woman died in the Infirmary.

　b　Sheila: Yes – except for all last summer, when you never came near me, and I wondered what had happened to you.

　c　Birling: … that I might find my way into the next Honours List. Just a knighthood, of course.

　d　Sheila: I caught sight of this girl smiling at Miss Francis – as if to say: 'Doesn't she look awful'.

　e　Sheila: Why – you fool – he knows. Of course he knows. And I hate to think how much he knows that we don't know yet.

　f　Birling: I went down myself and told them to clear out. And this girl, Eva Smith, was one of them.

　g　Inspector: I said she changed her name to Daisy Renton.

# 5 Truth and lies

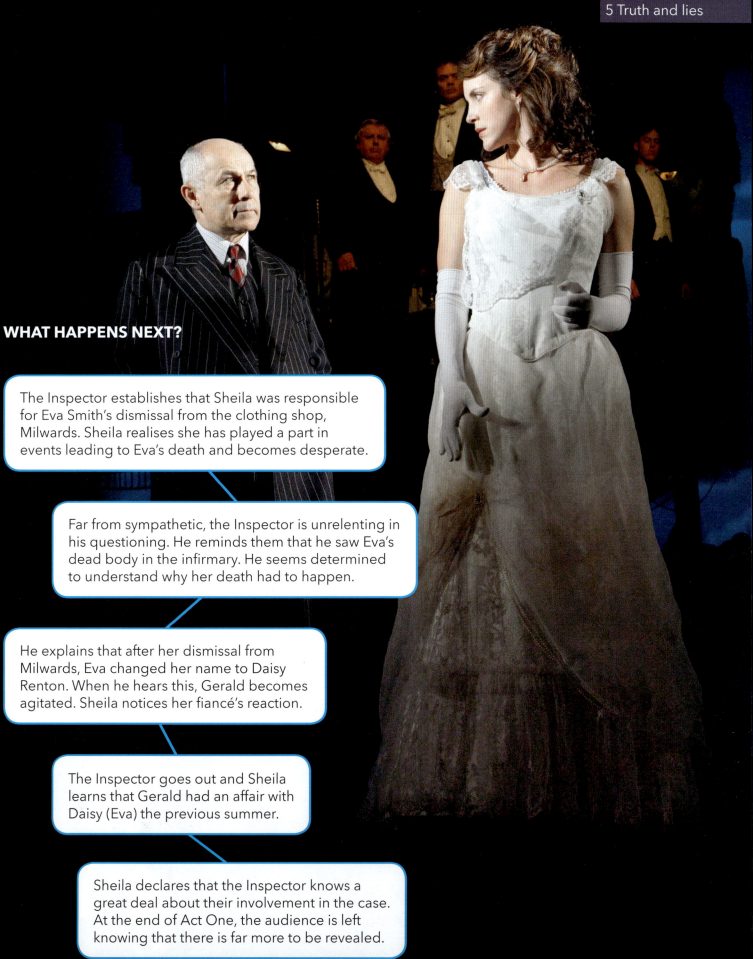

## WHAT HAPPENS NEXT?

The Inspector establishes that Sheila was responsible for Eva Smith's dismissal from the clothing shop, Milwards. Sheila realises she has played a part in events leading to Eva's death and becomes desperate.

Far from sympathetic, the Inspector is unrelenting in his questioning. He reminds them that he saw Eva's dead body in the infirmary. He seems determined to understand why her death had to happen.

He explains that after her dismissal from Milwards, Eva changed her name to Daisy Renton. When he hears this, Gerald becomes agitated. Sheila notices her fiancé's reaction.

The Inspector goes out and Sheila learns that Gerald had an affair with Daisy (Eva) the previous summer.

Sheila declares that the Inspector knows a great deal about their involvement in the case. At the end of Act One, the audience is left knowing that there is far more to be revealed.

# The Inspector's questions

There are several different types of question.

| Question type | Explanation | Example |
| --- | --- | --- |
| closed question | can usually be answered with one or two words | Did you have a good day? Yes. |
| open question | to encourage longer and fuller answers | What have you been doing today? |
| funnel question | moves from general to more specific questions | Tell me about your lunch hour. Who did you meet? What did you talk about? What was the most memorable thing they said? |
| probing question | follows on from a main question to try to find out more | When they said that to you, what went through your mind? |
| leading question | suggests that the questioner knows what the answer will be | I don't suppose you'll be wanting any more ice-cream, then? |
| rhetorical question | used to make a point, without expecting or needing an answer | Do you realise how late you are? |

1. What types of questions does the Inspector use in this section of the play? Write down examples of as many different types as you can find.

2. For each example you find, write a short paragraph explaining its effect. For example:

> The Inspector says, 'In fact, in a kind of way, you might be said to have been jealous of her.' This is a leading question. He is trying to get Sheila to admit that her actions towards Eva were selfish and therefore that she has played a part in this girl's death. It stops Sheila in her tracks and shakes her confidence. We start to see a different side to Sheila's character.

## D'you mind if I give myself a drink, Sheila?

*Gerald: Act One*

## PUTTING DETAILS TO USE

Read the following extract then do the activities that follow. They will help you investigate the Inspector's **character** and consider how the writing builds **characterisation**. They will also help you to analyse the language he uses.

| | |
|---|---|
| **Inspector** | In fact, in a kind of way, you might be said to have been jealous of her. |
| **Sheila** | Yes, I suppose so. |
| **Inspector** | And so you used the power you had, as a daughter of a good customer and also of a man well known in the town, to punish the girl just because she made you feel like that? |
| **Sheila** | Yes, but it didn't seem to be anything very terrible at the time. Don't you understand? And if I could help her now, I would— |
| **Inspector** | (*harshly*) Yes, but you can't. It's too late. She's dead. |
| **Eric** | My God, it's a bit thick, when you come to think of it— |
| **Sheila** | (*stormily*) Oh shut up, Eric. I know, I know. It's the only time I've ever done anything like that, and I'll never, never do it again to anybody. I've noticed them giving me a sort of look sometimes at Milwards – I noticed it even this afternoon – and I suppose some of them remember. I feel now I can never go there again. Oh – why had this to happen? |
| **Inspector** | (*sternly*) That's what I asked myself tonight when I was looking at that dead girl. And then I said to myself: 'Well, we'll try to understand why it had to happen.' And that's why I'm here, and why I'm not going until I know all that happened. Eva Smith lost her job with Birling and Company because the strike failed and they were determined not to have another one. At last she found another job – under what name I don't know – in a big shop, and had to leave there because you were annoyed with yourself and passed the annoyance on to her. Now she had to try something else. So first she changed her name to Daisy Renton – |
| **Gerald** | (*startled*) What? |
| **Inspector** | (*steadily*) I said she changed her name to Daisy Renton. |
| **Gerald** | (*pulling himself together*) D'you mind if I give myself a drink, Sheila? |
| | SHEILA *merely nods, still staring at him, and he goes across to the tantalus on the sideboard for a whisky.* |
| **Inspector** | Where is your father, Miss Birling? |
| **Sheila** | He went into the drawing-room, to tell my mother what was happening here. Eric, take the Inspector along to the drawing-room. |
| | As ERIC *moves, the* INSPECTOR *looks from* SHEILA *to* GERALD, *then goes out with* ERIC. |
| | Well, Gerald? |

## How does the Inspector question Sheila?

For the following activities, either work by yourself, writing down brief answers, or discuss the questions in small groups. If you work in groups, keep notes of your discussion.

**1** Answer the following questions:

   a  Why does the Inspector suggest that Sheila is jealous of Eva Smith?

   b  'It's too late. She's dead.' Why does the Inspector use such short sentences here and why does he place the word 'dead' at the end of his speech?

**2** Find three examples from the extract where Sheila shows her insecurity. Write a paragraph explaining how you think the Inspector exploits Sheila's insecurity.

**3** The Inspector's language is usually matter-of-fact and unemotional. Identify three examples of this in the extract.

**4** Why do you think the Inspector gives such a long summary of Eva Smith's story?

## What effect do the Inspector's questions have?

**1** Why do you think the Inspector ends his story with the name 'Daisy Renton'? List three points about the effect this has on Gerald.

**2** Why do you think Priestley writes the stage direction, 'the INSPECTOR looks from SHEILA to GERALD, then goes out with ERIC'? What effect does it have?

**3** The Inspector causes conflict amongst the other characters without ever losing his temper. Find two examples of where he does this.

**4** What do you think Priestley wants the audience to think about the Inspector at this point in the play? Write a short paragraph explaining your ideas.

**5** At the end of Act One, Gerald says, 'I don't come into this suicide business'. With a partner, talk about how Gerald might have some responsibility for the suicide.

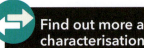
Find out more about character and characterisation in the play in Unit 13.

## The structure of the play

**1** The play is structured so that, one by one, each character is shown to have some responsibility for the death of Eva Smith. Create a spider diagram to record your notes about the effect this structure has on the audience.

**2** Look at the stage directions at the end of Act One:

*She looks at him almost in triumph. He looks crushed. The door slowly opens and the* INSPECTOR *appears, looking steadily and searchingly at them.*

The look between Gerald and Sheila is a dramatic device that tells us something about the way their relationship is changing. Write a short paragraph explaining how the relationship is changing.

**3** At the end of the act, the Inspector returns. Why might Priestley have chosen to end the first act in this way? Look at the following examples of student responses to this question. Which student best sums up Priestley's reasons for ending the act in this way? Explain your choice.

**Student A** Sheila and Gerald are in conflict. The tension in the act has built and we know that Gerald has been unfaithful to Sheila. We have reached the *climax* of Act One and we know that in Act Two there will be a huge row between Sheila and Gerald.

**Student B** By bringing the Inspector back into the room, Priestley ends the act on a *cliff-hanger*. We have witnessed Gerald and Sheila in conflict and know that Gerald has lied. We want to know more and we know from the way the Inspector has questioned other characters that when he says, 'Well?' his authority will ensure we will find out more in Act Two. We wait in anticipation.

**Student C** Gerald says, 'So – for God's sake – don't say anything to the Inspector.' We now realise that Gerald has threatened Sheila. She will disappear from the action and Gerald will probably turn out to be a murderer.

 Find out more about plot and structure in the play in Unit 11.

 **Learning checkpoint**

The Inspector's questioning has led Sheila to think carefully about the consequences of her actions and how she might have played a part in Eva's death. However, she remains defensive, claiming that it is the only time she has ever done anything like this.

Write Sheila's diary entry for the day she visited Milwards, describing what happened. Think about these questions:

- Would she write about the event in the same way she told the story to the Inspector?
- Does she consider the consequences of her actions at the time or when she gets home?
- Does she feel bad about her behaviour or is she still angry and jealous?

 **Key terms**

**climax:** the high point and most dramatic moment in a scene, act or play.

**cliff-hanger:** the end of an episode or an instalment when something surprising happens, so people will want to find out what happens next.

It's too late. She's dead.

*Inspector: Act One*

## GETTING IT INTO WRITING

### Writing about the Inspector

Look at this writing task:

**How does Priestley present the character of the Inspector in this part of the play?**

① Use the notes you have made in this unit to help you plan a response to the task. Remember:

- When you look at **character**, you are thinking about the Inspector as a person.
- When you look at **characterisation**, you are thinking about how the playwright presents that character to an audience.

First write your notes as a spider diagram or a list of bullet points. Swap your notes with a partner and structure your partner's notes into an order for an essay plan. Do this by giving each idea a number.

② Think of a direct and relevant way to start your essay (do not begin with 'In this essay I am going to …'). Then write the first paragraph.

  a   Swap your opening paragraph with a partner. With a different coloured pen, highlight any words in your partner's work that you feel are unnecessary. Be honest!
  b   Swap back. Do you agree with what your partner has highlighted?

③ Write the rest of the essay with your partner: one of you is the thinker, the other is the scribe. A tells B what to write. After 15 minutes, swap over. When you have finished, spend five minutes checking back over what you have written.

 **Complete this assignment on Cambridge Elevate.**

# 5 Truth and lies

### Learning checkpoint

**How will I know I've done this well?**

✔ **The best answers** will show knowledge by putting the episode in the context of the developing plot. They will show good analytical skills by exploring how Priestley presents the Inspector. They will show good interpretative skills by commenting on characterisation and **setting**. They will offer personal interpretation based on evidence from the text.

✔ **Good answers** will demonstrate a knowledge and clear understanding of the Inspector's character. They will use well-chosen examples from the extract and refer to other events in the play. They will offer personal interpretations.

✔ **Weaker answers** will only comment on the events. They will tend to recount the plot rather than interpret the evidence. They will comment on characters as real people, rather than how they are created by Priestley.

## GETTING FURTHER

### Compare Inspectors

Unusually for a character in fiction, the character of the Inspector does not develop in the course of the play. We know no more about him at the end than we do at the beginning. As you read and study the play, look closely at the role of the Inspector and think about his function in the drama.

1. Compare the characters of the Inspector and Sheila. In what ways are they different?

2. Some people have observed that the Inspector is rather like Priestley himself – directing and controlling the action. Do you think this is true? Explain the reasons for your answer.

3. Read any of the original Sherlock Holmes novels by Sir Arthur Conan Doyle, such as *The Hound of the Baskervilles*, or watch a film or television **adaptation**. What similarities are there between Sherlock Holmes and the Inspector?

4. Watch an episode of any TV crime drama of your choice. How does the characterisation of the central investigator compare to Priestley's Inspector?

Watch some actors discuss the Inspector on Cambridge Elevate.

# 6

## Appearance and reality

How does Priestley develop Gerald's character?

Your progress in this unit:
- understand and explore Gerald's character
- develop ideas about the theme of appearance and reality
- Produce a piece of writing from Gerald's point of view
- use an essay plan to write about the theme of appearance and reality
- develop a response to writing tasks.

## GETTING STARTED – THE PLAY AND YOU

### First impressions

**1** Work in pairs. Discuss the following questions.

  a  How important to you are first impressions of people?
  b  How do you form an impression of someone when you first meet them? What things do you notice?
  c  Can you think of people in the news or from history who turn out to be different from the first impressions people have had of them?

**2** Gerald is good at putting on an appearance, but the Inspector sees through this.

  a  Should you always try to be yourself at all times?
  b  Are there any situations where it is right or acceptable to give the impression that you are someone you are not?

## GETTING CLOSER – FOCUS ON DETAILS

### Understanding Gerald

Read the play from the beginning of Act Two to where Gerald describes how he met Daisy Renton up to the line '**She agreed at once.**'

What Gerald says, what he thinks and what he does are often quite different. He appears to be a well-spoken, well-educated young man with wealthy parents. He knows how to behave and he has certainly created a good impression on Arthur Birling. He knows how to present himself to the world.

Read the following extract, then do the activities that follow.

## 6 Appearance and reality

## WHAT HAPPENS NEXT?

At the beginning of Act Two, Gerald asks the Inspector if Sheila can be excused from further questioning, but Sheila refuses to go. Gerald and Sheila argue.

The Inspector explains why Sheila should stay – she now feels responsible for Eva's suicide and if she does not hear any more of the questioning she will be alone with her responsibility. He says that '**we will all have to share our guilt.**'

Mrs Birling comes into the room and says she will be glad to tell the Inspector anything he wants to know, but she seems irritated and does not think she will be able to help with much. Sheila warns her mother not to say something she will later regret.

Mrs Birling treats Sheila as if she is a child, and we also see her superior attitude towards Eva and the Inspector. She reminds the Inspector that her husband was lord mayor.

The Inspector turns his questioning to Gerald and asks him when he first met Daisy Renton (Eva Smith). Mr and Mrs Birling are shocked to discover that Gerald knew the girl. Gerald admits that he met Daisy in a bar at the music hall.

Sheila becomes suspicious and then angry as she realises Gerald has been deceiving her. Gerald tells the story as if his only intention was to rescue Eva from Alderman Meggarty.

**Gerald**  I happened to look in, one night, after a long dull day, and as the show wasn't very bright, I went down into the bar for a drink. It's a favourite haunt of women of the town—

**Mrs B.**  Women of the town?

**Birling**  Yes, yes. But I see no point in mentioning the subject – especially – (*indicating* SHEILA.)

**Mrs B.**  It would be much better if Sheila didn't listen to this story at all.

**Sheila**  But you're forgetting I'm supposed to be engaged to the hero of it. Go on, Gerald. You went down into the bar, which is a favourite haunt of women of the town.

**Gerald**  I'm glad I amuse you—

**Inspector**  (*sharply*) Come along, Mr Croft. What happened?

**Gerald**  I didn't propose to stay long down there. I hate those hard-eyed dough-faced women. But then I noticed a girl who looked quite different. She was very pretty – soft brown hair and big dark eyes—(*breaks off.*) My God!

**Inspector**  What's the matter?

**Gerald**  (*distressed*) Sorry – I – well, I've suddenly realized – taken it in properly – that she's dead—

**Inspector**  (*harshly*) Yes, she's dead.

**Sheila**  And probably between us we killed her.

**Mrs B.**  (*sharply*) Sheila, don't talk nonsense.

**Sheila**  You wait, Mother.

**Inspector**  (*To* GERALD) Go on.

**Gerald**  She looked young and fresh and charming and altogether out of place down there. And obviously she wasn't enjoying herself. Old Joe Meggarty, half-drunk and goggle-eyed, had wedged her into a corner with that obscene fat carcass of his—

**Mrs B.**  (*cutting in*) There's no need to be disgusting. And surely you don't mean Alderman Meggarty?

**Gerald**  Of course I do. He's a notorious womanizer as well as being one of the worst sots and rogues in Brumley—

**Inspector**  Quite right.

**Mrs B.**  (*staggered*) Well, really! Alderman Meggarty! I must say, we are learning something tonight.

**Sheila**  (*coolly*) Of course we are. But everybody knows about that horrible old Meggarty. A girl I know had to see him at the Town Hall one afternoon and she only escaped with a torn blouse—

**Birling** (*sharply, shocked*) Sheila!

**Inspector** (*to* GERALD) Go on, please.

**Gerald** The girl saw me looking at her and then gave me a glance that was nothing less than a cry for help. So I went across and told Joe Meggarty some nonsense – that the manager had a message for him or something like that – got him out of the way – and then told the girl that if she didn't want any more of that sort of thing, she'd better let me take her out of there. She agreed at once.

---

**1** This activity helps you explore Gerald's character and the thoughts behind what he says (the **subtext**). Work in groups.

- **a** Decide who will play each **character** and read the extract through until you are confident with it.
- **b** Perform the scene to another group. At any moment, someone watching can call 'Stop'.
- **c** The action then freezes and that person asks one of the characters a question – for example 'Gerald, why did you emphasise the word "happened" when you said, "I happened to look in"?'
- **d** The actor playing the character must answer the question in role, considering what might be going through that character's mind – for example: 'Well I suppose I didn't want to give the impression that I'm the kind of man who regularly goes to that sort of place.'
- **e** The questioner can interrogate further if they are not happy with the answer – for example: 'Exactly how many times have you been there in the last two weeks?'
- **f** When the questioner is satisfied with the answer, they say 'Go' and the actors continue reading the scene from the point where the action was frozen.

### Learning checkpoint

**1** Use your exploration of Gerald's character to list seven bullet points about Gerald. For example:

- Gerald is a wealthy member of the aristocracy. His mother and father are Lord and Lady Croft. He will one day inherit this title.
- He is about to be engaged to Sheila Birling. It appears that her parents are very excited about this arrangement …

**2** Use your bullet points to write two or three paragraphs about Gerald's character.

### Key terms

**subtext:** the unspoken thoughts and motives of a character in a play or novel.

GCSE English Literature for AQA: An Inspector Calls

## PUTTING DETAILS TO USE

### Reading between the lines

A character is often more interesting if what they say is not always what they mean or what they think. Priestley uses this idea in the character of Gerald.

**1** Read the extract again. What do you learn from it about Gerald's lifestyle? Discuss this in pairs.

**2** Gerald breaks off his story by saying '**My God**' and becoming distressed. Why do you think he does this? Rank the following reasons according to how well you think they explain his behaviour at this point.

  a   He is genuinely upset by what has happened.
  b   He realises that Sheila is listening and does not want to arouse her suspicion.
  c   He wants to seem innocent and caring in front of the Inspector.
  d   He feels guilty for what has happened to Daisy.

**3** a  Why do you think Gerald describes the women in the bar as '**hard-eyed**' and '**dough-faced**'?
   b  He contrasts this with Daisy's '**soft brown hair and big dark eyes**'. What effect does this use of language have?

**4** Look at this speech and list the words Gerald uses that emphasise how unpleasant Joe Meggarty is:

> She looked young and fresh and charming and altogether out of place down there. And obviously she wasn't enjoying herself. Old Joe Meggarty, half-drunk and goggle-eyed, had wedged her into a corner with that obscene fat carcass of his.

> But you're forgetting I'm supposed to be engaged to the hero of it.
>
> *Sheila: Act Two*

**5** Look at the language Gerald uses in his last speech. He uses phrases such as:

> a glance that was nothing less than a cry for help

> … told the girl that if she didn't want any more of that sort of thing, she'd better let me take her out of there.

Write a paragraph explaining what impression Gerald is trying to give of himself. Use one of the quotations as evidence.

## Other characters' perspectives

Sheila is very quick to comment on Gerald's story:

> … you're forgetting I'm supposed to be engaged to the hero of it. Go on, Gerald. You went down into the bar, which is a favourite haunt of women of the town.

**1** Create a spider diagram with 'What Sheila didn't know about Gerald' written in the middle. Note down all the things that Sheila discovers about Gerald in this part of the play.

**2** Mrs Birling seems unaware of several things:

- She is surprised by Alderman Meggarty's behaviour.
- She does not realise that Eric drinks heavily.
- She does not understand that the Inspector may ask her difficult questions.
- She is shocked to discover that Gerald knew Daisy Renton.

What does this suggest about her?

**3** When Gerald seems upset about what happened to Daisy, the Inspector says, **'Yes, she's dead.'** What does this imply about his attitude towards Gerald?

## Gerald's diary

**1** Use the ideas you have collected about Gerald's character to write his diary entry for the evening he met Daisy Renton. Include some details of his everyday life, and his thoughts and reflections about his actions. Remember, he might not always be truthful – even to himself! You could begin:

> Gosh. What a long day. I had to go and get a suit fitted in town and afterwards I was …

 **Learning checkpoint**

How has Priestley developed Gerald's character from the beginning of the play until this point? Write one or two paragraphs to show Gerald's character development. Use the notes you have made so far in this unit to help you. Make sure you use at least one quotation as evidence.

**How will I know I've done this well?**

✔ Include your own interpretations.
✔ Support your interpretations by referring to detail in the text.
✔ Explore Priestley's **characterisation** of Gerald.
✔ Write in well-organised paragraphs.
✔ Use accurate spelling and clear, well-punctuated sentences.

 **Read more about character and characterisation in the play in Unit 13.**

## GETTING IT INTO WRITING

### Plan an essay on Gerald

In this unit, you have explored Gerald's words and actions in detail.

**1** In pairs, discuss how Priestley presents the character of Gerald in this part of the play. Think about what Gerald says and how others react to him.

**2** Look at this list of points that a student has started to write down, in no particular order, for an answer to this question about Gerald. Put these points into an order and think of some more to form an essay plan.

- Give evidence for Gerald as a respectable young man.
- Explain his use of 'hard-eyed' and 'dough faced'.
- Gerald's character as an example of presenting Priestley's ideas about appearance and reality.
- Explain our first impressions of Gerald as a respectable young man.
- Priestley is suggesting that people might not always be what they appear to be.
- Refer to some of the words Gerald uses to make his actions seem heroic.

**3** Now write the first two paragraphs of your answer to this question. Use the plan to help you.

**Complete this assignment on Cambridge Elevate.**

## GETTING FURTHER

### Impressions of Gerald

**1** As you read the rest of the play, think about how Gerald's character develops. Compare his journey with that of Eric and Sheila. What does he learn?

**2** In this unit, you have considered the theme of appearance and reality. Most of the characters in the play are not what they at first appear to be. Think about the character of Gerald in the play so far. Create a spider diagram to record notes about your first impressions of Gerald's character.

    **a** What image do you have of Gerald (you might think about his looks, clothes, accent and background)? Add some notes to your diagram.

    **b** How are these first impressions altered by what you have learnt about him since the beginning of the play?

**3** Use the same technique to understand your first impressions of other characters, such as Eric, Birling, Sheila or Mrs Birling, and how these change as the play progresses.

6 Appearance and reality

Old Joe Meggarty, half-drunk and goggle-eyed, had wedged her into a corner with that obscene fat carcass of his.

*Gerald: Act Two*

# 7

## Duty and downfall

**How does Priestley present Mrs Birling and the structure of the play?**

Your progress in this unit:
- understand and explain the character of Mrs Birling
- explore the way she brings about her own downfall
- investigate the way the action is brought to a climax at the end of Act Two
- organise your investigations into a piece of writing under timed conditions
- develop a response to writing tasks.

### GETTING STARTED – THE PLAY AND YOU

#### Eva's dilemma

**1** An 18-year-old girl becomes pregnant. She had told her partner that she was using contraception. After some careful thought, she decides that she wants to keep the child. Her family think this is the wrong decision and they refuse to help her.

Discuss the following statements in pairs or groups. Show how far you agree or disagree with each statement by choosing a number between 1 and 10, where 1 = strongly disagree and 10 = strongly agree.

a It's her own fault – she should have been more careful. She is entirely responsible.
b She should have to pay for the upbringing of the child herself.
c The father should be traced and made to pay to look after the baby.
d She should be given money by the state to help provide for herself and the child.
e The authorities should take the baby from her and look after it.
f She should go to charities for help.

**2** a How do the views held by Mrs Birling about Eva's pregnancy compare to the views of society today?
b If Eva and Eric were real people living in the 21st century, how might they be affected by the pregnancy?

### GETTING CLOSER – FOCUS ON DETAILS

#### What happens in this section?

Look at the summary, then read the play from the end of the extract in Unit 6 to the end of Act Two. Then answer the questions that follow.

# WHAT HAPPENS NEXT?

**7 Duty and downfall**

- Gerald reveals the details of his relationship with Daisy Renton in front of Mr Birling, Mrs Birling and Sheila.

- They discover that Daisy lived in a flat belonging to Gerald's friend, and Gerald provided money for her. She was his mistress until he broke it off.

- The Inspector explains that Daisy went away for two months and kept a diary.

- Sheila hands back the ring to Gerald saying that '**you and I aren't the same people**'. She realises that she, her father and Gerald all have some responsibility for the death of Eva Smith.

- The Inspector questions Mrs Birling. She tells him that Eva Smith had come to her charitable committee asking for assistance. Eva called herself Mrs Birling. She was pregnant and needed money. The father of her child had offered her some money but she had refused to take it because she knew it was stolen.

- Mrs Birling instructed her committee to refuse to give Eva any money. In her opinion, the young girl should look after herself and the father should provide for her: '**If, as she said, he didn't belong to her class, and was some drunken young idler, then that's all the more reason why he shouldn't escape.**' She believes he should be made an example of and that the girl's suicide is down to him.

- Sheila tries to stop her mother from saying any more, but Mrs Birling continues to blame the father. Just before the curtain falls, she realises that the father is, in fact, Eric – her own son.

## What does Gerald really mean?

Re-read the part of the text where Gerald tells the story of his relationship with Daisy Renton.

**1** Copy the table and complete it by putting the following explanations next to the correct quotations.

- a The Inspector is blunt in his questioning, stating what Gerald is reluctant to acknowledge.
- b Gerald seems ready to accept some responsibility in the same way Sheila has done earlier.
- c Priestley gives us some **exposition**, which helps the audience understand that Eva had no one to rely on.
- d Gerald was the one who ended the relationship, suggesting that he was always in control.
- e Sheila is beginning to understand things about her fiancé that she has never realised before.
- f Gerald is trying to excuse himself from his responsibility in a tragic suicide.

| Quotation | Explanation |
|---|---|
| 'She told me her name was Daisy Renton, that she'd lost both parents, that she originally came from somewhere outside Brumley.' | |
| 'And then you decided to keep her – as your mistress?' | |
| 'You were the wonderful Fairy Prince. You must have adored it, Gerald.' | |
| 'So I broke it off definitely before I went.' | |
| 'She didn't blame me at all. I wish to God she had now.' | |
| 'She told me she'd been happier than she'd ever been before.' | |

## PUTTING DETAILS TO USE

### Mrs Birling's story

When the Inspector asks his **rhetorical question** 'There was a meeting of the interviewing committee two weeks ago?', Mrs Birling replies evasively, saying 'I dare say there was'.

**1** Which of the following reasons do you think best explains her answer?

- a She wasn't there.
- b She can't remember.
- c She knows that the Inspector is going to ask her some difficult questions.
- d She is worried about Sheila and does not want the questioning to continue.

**2** Which of the following statements about Mrs Birling's story of Eva's visit to the Brumley Women's Charity are true and which are false?

- a Eva Smith called herself Miss Birling when she came.
- b Eva Smith was pregnant.
- c Mrs Birling knew that Eric was the father of Eva's child.
- d Mrs Birling believed that the father should provide for the child.

### Key terms

**exposition:** a detailed explanation of a situation or event.

**rhetorical question:** a question intended to make a point rather than requiring an answer.

## Mrs Birling's attitudes

We've selected this extract to help you develop your understanding of the play and so that you can have more confidence to use textual evidence in your written responses.

**Mrs B.** […] He should be made an example of. If the girl's death is due to anybody, then it's due to him.

**Inspector** And if her story is true – that he was stealing money—

**Mrs B.** (*rather agitated now*) There's no point in assuming that—

**Inspector** But suppose we do, what then?

**Mrs B.** Then he'd be entirely responsible – because the girl wouldn't have come to us, and have been refused assistance, if it hadn't been for him—

**Inspector** So he's the chief culprit anyhow.

**Mrs B.** Certainly. And he ought to be dealt with very severely—

**Sheila** (*with sudden alarm*) Mother – stop – stop!

**Birling** Be quiet, Sheila!

**Sheila** But don't you see—

**Mrs B.** (*severely*) You're behaving like an hysterical child tonight.

SHEILA *begins crying quietly.* MRS BIRLING *turns to* INSPECTOR.

And if you'd take some steps to find this young man and then make sure that he's compelled to confess in public his responsibility – instead of staying here asking quite unnecessary questions – then you really would be doing your duty.

**Inspector** (*grimly*) Don't worry, Mrs Birling. I shall do my duty. (*He looks at his watch.*)

**Mrs B.** (*triumphantly*) I'm glad to hear it.

**Inspector** No hushing up, eh? Make an example of the young man, eh? Public confession of responsibility – um?

**Mrs B.** Certainly. I consider it your duty. And now no doubt you'd like to say good night.

**Inspector** Not yet. I'm waiting.

**Mrs B.** Waiting for what?

**Inspector** To do my duty.

**Sheila** (*distressed*) Now, Mother – don't you see?

**Mrs B.** (*understanding now*) But surely … I mean … it's ridiculous …

*She stops, and exchanges a frightened glance with her husband.*

**Birling** (*terrified now*) Look Inspector, you're not trying to tell us that – that my boy – is mixed up in this—?

**Inspector** (*sternly*) If he is, then we know what to do, don't we? Mrs Birling has just told us.

| | |
|---|---|
| **Birling** | (*thunderstruck*) My God! But – look here— |
| **Mrs B.** | (*agitated*) I don't believe it. I *won't* believe it … |
| **Sheila** | Mother – I begged you and begged you to stop— |

> INSPECTOR *holds up a hand. We hear the front door. They wait, looking towards door.* ERIC *enters, looking extremely pale and distressed. He meets their inquiring stares.*
>
> *Curtain falls quickly.*

---

**1** Make a list of the words in the extract that suggest Mrs Birling is certain in her beliefs.

**2** **a** Choose two quotations from the extract that reveal Mrs Birling's attitude towards her daughter.
 **b** Write a sentence for each quotation, explaining its significance.

**3** Write a paragraph about Mrs Birling's attitude towards Eva Smith and the father of her child. Use the following points to help you. Find at least one quotation from the extract to support your comments.

 **a** She thinks the father should be responsible for looking after the mother and child.
 **b** If he does not, Mrs Birling thinks he should be dealt with severely.
 **c** She does not think Eva has a right to expect help from anyone else.

**4** At what point in the extract does Mrs Birling finally realise who the father of the child is?

**5** What is the significance of '**the frightened glance**' Mrs Birling gives her husband in the development of her **character**? Discuss this with a partner.

### ✓ Learning checkpoint

**1** Write two or three paragraphs describing what we learn about Mrs Birling's attitudes and perspectives in this section of the play.

**2** Write two or three paragraphs about how Sheila's attitude towards her mother changes.

In your answers, think about how Mrs Birling refuses to change her attitude and how Sheila's attitudes are changing. You should:

- ✔ show how Priestley presents the character of Mrs Birling, her attitudes and perspectives
- ✔ explore Sheila's changing perspective of her family and Gerald
- ✔ give a personal interpretation about the characters of Mrs Birling and Sheila
- ✔ use good spelling, punctuation and grammar
- ✔ use evidence from the text to support the points you make.

# 7 Duty and downfall

## The Inspector's language

**1** Look at what the Inspector says in the extract. Write one sentence for each of the following lines to explain the effect of the language he uses.

a   'And if her story is true – that he was stealing money …'
b   'But suppose we do, what then?'
c   'So he's the chief culprit anyhow.'
d   '(*grimly*) Don't worry, Mrs Birling. I shall do my duty. (*He looks at his watch.*)'
e   'No hushing up, eh? Make an example of the young man, eh? Public confession of responsibility – um?'
f   '(*sternly*) If he is, then we know what to do, don't we? Mrs Birling has just told us.'

 Find out more about language in the play in Unit 15.

## Dramatic irony

Playwrights often use **dramatic irony** to build the drama in their plays, and Priestley uses it to great effect in this extract. For example Mrs Birling says:

He should be made an example of. If the girl's death is due to anybody, then it's due to him.

At this point, she is unaware that the father of the child is her own son, Eric. The audience, however, has already worked this out. They are one step ahead of Mrs Birling.

**1** Write a paragraph explaining the effect of dramatic irony in the play so far. Begin:

Dramatic irony makes the play interesting for the audience because …

## A dramatic ending

**1** Act Two ends with Eric returning to the stage. Discuss these questions in small groups.

a   Why do you think Priestley has chosen to end the act with Eric's return?
b   Why doesn't Priestley give him anything to say at this point?
c   What does the audience know that Eric does not know?
d   How does the end of Act Two prepare the audience for the next act?

 **Key terms**

**dramatic irony:** when the audience knows something that a character on stage is unaware of.

Don't worry, Mrs Birling. I shall do my duty.

*Inspector: Act Two*

GCSE English Literature for AQA: An Inspector Calls

## GETTING IT INTO WRITING

### Writing about the end of Act Two

**1** Think about how Priestley brings the action to a **climax** at the end of Act Two. Choose two of these points and write 150 words about each one:

- why Eric is out of the room **and** Eric's return to the room
- how the Inspector makes Mrs Birling condemn her own son
- how Priestley builds up tension
- the role of Sheila in the scene.

Complete this assignment on Cambridge Elevate.

Watch some actors discussing the end of Act Two on Cambridge Elevate.

### Learning checkpoint

**How will I know I've done this well?**

✔ **The best answers** will show that you understand how Priestley has carefully structured events so they reach a dramatic climax at the end of Act Two. You will write about, for example, Mrs Birling's hypocritical attitudes to the father, and how these are drawn out by the Inspector's manipulative questioning. You will also comment on how Priestley raises the tension through Sheila's interjections and Eric's return.

✔ **Good answers** will show a clear understanding of the characters and the ideas they represent. Comments about Mrs Birling's attitudes to the father, for example, will be backed up with well-chosen quotations. You will comment on specific words or phrases used in the text. You will use accurate spelling and clear, well-punctuated sentences.

✔ **Weaker answers** will comment on the events in general, using few or no specific examples and without mentioning why Priestley might structure them to have an impact on the audience.

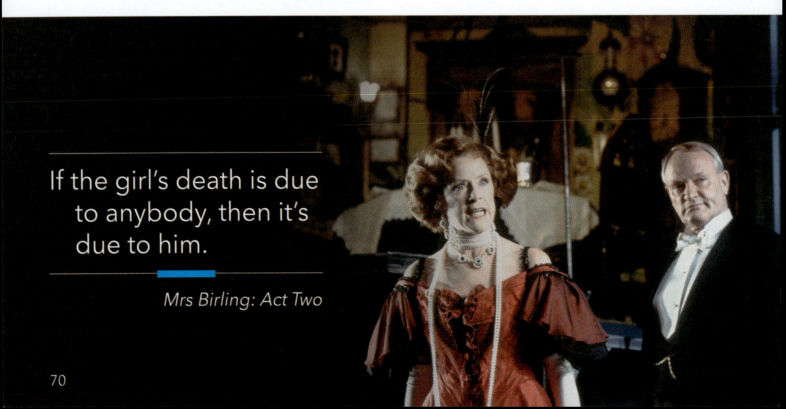

> If the girl's death is due to anybody, then it's due to him.
>
> *Mrs Birling: Act Two*

## GETTING FURTHER

### Gender stereotypes

Gender stereotyping means using simplified and general ideas about the differences between men and women. For example Birling assumes that Sheila will not work for the family firm because she is a woman.

**1** There are four women in the play: Mrs Birling, Sheila, Edna and Eva. Copy and complete the following table to show the different female **stereotypes** that are represented by each of these characters.

| Character | Gender stereotype |
|---|---|
| Mrs Birling | |
| Sheila | |
| Edna | |
| Eva Smith | |

**2** Create a similar table to comment on the attitudes to male stereotypes presented in the play. What different male stereotypes are represented by:

a  Arthur Birling
b  Eric
c  Gerald
d  the Inspector?

**3** Even though the play was set in 1912, it presents attitudes that people still held in 1945, when it was written. To what extent have these stereotypes changed today?

### Writing about structure

**1** Use what you have learnt about structure to write a short script for an ending to an act for your own play. Try to build towards a climax at the end of your act so you leave your audience wanting to know what happens next.

Choose one of these plot structures as the starting point for your script:

a  A man and a woman argue; one walks out …
b  A mother and daughter argue because the daughter thinks that the mother is wearing inappropriate clothes …
c  Two members of the school rock band argue about the direction their music should be taking …

# 8 Parents and problems

How does Priestley present conflict between the generations?

Your progress in this unit:
- explore and characterise the relationship between Eric and Birling
- explore the conflict between the older and younger generations
- write about the relationships between parents and their children within the Birling family.

## GETTING STARTED – THE PLAY AND YOU

### Generation gap

Discuss the following questions in a small group, or make your own notes and discuss them with a partner. You could create spider diagrams to help you.

1. Why do the older and younger generations argue so much?
2. What are the main differences in attitudes and outlook between the younger and older generation?
3. How much do you think we are influenced by our childhood and upbringing?
4. What kind of father do you think Eric would have been?

## GETTING CLOSER – FOCUS ON DETAILS

### The conflict between the generations

Look at the summary, then read from the beginning of Act Three to the point where the Inspector intervenes between Birling and Eric ('**Stop!**').

One of the key themes in the play is the conflict between the generations. This is represented in the family by the rift between Mr and Mrs Birling – who want to keep things the way they have always been – and Sheila, who is led by the Inspector into questioning their attitudes. Eric is also drawn towards the idea of change. The argument builds until Birling seems to be about to hit Eric. The Inspector intervenes to stop him. This incident suggests the kind of father Birling has been.

1. Identify any quotations from this section of the play that illustrate the conflict between the generations.
2. When Eric tells the story of his relationship with Eva, his language suggests that things were not clear to him: '**And I didn't even remember – that's the hellish thing**'.
   a. Identify two other examples of Eric's uncertainty about the situation.
   b. What does this suggest about his relationship with Eva?

## WHAT HAPPENS NEXT?

8 Parents and problems

At the start of Act Three, Eric realises that the family knows about his relationship with Eva. Sheila says that she has told her mother tonight about his drinking, but reminds Eric that she could have told her months ago.

Eric admits to having had a sexual relationship with Eva after meeting her at the Palace bar, although he says, 'I wasn't in love with her or anything'.

Birling orders Sheila to take her mother out of the room. Eric says that later Eva told him she was going to have a baby. '**She didn't want me to marry her. Said I didn't love her – and all that.**' As she didn't have a job, Eric insisted on giving her 50 pounds, which he stole from the office of the family firm.

Sheila comes back into the room. Birling becomes very agitated about getting the money back and wants to cover it up in the accounts.

Sheila and the Inspector tell Eric that Eva had been to his mother's committee and that his mother refused to help her. Eric is angry and accuses his mother of having killed Eva and the child she would have had – his child and her own grandchild.

73

## Father and son

We've selected this extract to help you develop your understanding of the play and so that you can have more confidence to use textual evidence in your written responses.

**Mrs B.** (*shocked*) Eric! You stole money?

**Eric** No, not really. I intended to pay it back.

**Birling** We've heard that story before. How could you have paid it back?

**Eric** I'd have managed somehow. I had to have some money—

**Birling** I don't understand how you could take as much as that out of the office without somebody knowing.

**Eric** There were some small accounts to collect, and I asked for cash—

**Birling** Gave the firm's receipt and then kept the money, eh?

**Eric** Yes.

**Birling** You must give me a list of those accounts. I've got to cover this up as soon as I can. You damned fool – why didn't you come to me when you found yourself in this mess?

**Eric** Because you're not the kind of father a chap could go to when he's in trouble – that's why.

**Birling** (*angrily*) Don't talk to me like that. Your trouble is – you've been spoilt—

**Inspector** (*cutting in*) And my trouble is – that I haven't much time. You'll be able to divide the responsibility between you when I've gone. (*To* ERIC.) Just one last question, that's all. The girl discovered that this money you were giving her was stolen, didn't she?

**Eric** (*miserably*) Yes. That was the worst of all. She wouldn't take any more, and she didn't want to see me again. (*Sudden startled tone.*) Here, but how did you know that? Did she tell you?

**Inspector** No. She told me nothing. I never spoke to her.

**Sheila** She told mother.

**Mrs B.** (*alarmed*) Sheila!

**Sheila** Well, he has to know.

**Eric** (*to* MRS BIRLING) She told you? Did she come here – but then she couldn't have done, she didn't even know I lived here. What happened?

MRS BIRLING, *distressed, shakes her head but does not reply.*

Come on, don't just look like that. Tell me – tell me – what happened?

**Inspector** (*with calm authority*) I'll tell you. She went to your mother's committee for help, after she'd done with you. Your mother refused that help.

**Eric** (*nearly at breaking point*) Then – you killed her. She came to you to protect me – and you turned her away – yes, and you killed her – and the child she'd have had too – my child – your own grandchild – you killed them both – damn you, damn you—

**Mrs B.** (*very distressed now*) No – Eric – please – I didn't know – I didn't understand—

**Eric** (*almost threatening her*) You don't understand anything. You never did. You never even tried – you—

**Sheila** (*frightened*) Eric, don't – don't—

**Birling** (*furious, intervening*) Why, you hysterical young fool – get back – or I'll—

**Inspector** (*taking charge, masterfully*) Stop!

*They are suddenly quiet, staring at him.*

**8 Parents and problems**

**1** Write a paragraph describing how Priestley presents the relationship between Eric and Birling in this extract. Identify at least one quotation from the extract to support your comments.

**2** When Eric says he intended to pay the money back, Birling responds with **'We've heard that story before.'** Write a short paragraph to interrogate this quotation. Remember – when you 'interrogate' a quotation or an action, you look into the detail and ask searching questions. For example: 'What does this imply about the relationship between father and son?'

**3** Birling says: **'You must give me a list of those accounts. I've got to cover this up as soon as I can.'** Write a paragraph in the **first person** in which Birling explains his reasons for wanting to cover this up. You could begin like this:

*I can't believe this – my own son, my own flesh and blood. There will be a scandal because …*

**4** Eric says that Birling is **'not the kind of father a chap could go to when he's in trouble'**. Write three bullet points analysing why he says this. For example:

- The only way in which Birling speaks to Eric is to tell him off or express disappointment.

 Find out more about themes and ideas in the play in Unit 14.

You must give me a list of those accounts. I've got to cover this up as soon as I can.

*Birling: Act Three*

## Eric's role

**1** Eric says to his mother '**Then – you killed her.**' Write a paragraph exploring why this is a key moment in the play. You could begin like this:

*Since the beginning of the play we have seen that Eric is in conflict with his parents. This builds to the point when he accuses his own mother of murder. His statement is …*

**2** Eric says, '**You don't understand anything. You never did.**' What does this tell the audience about the family?

**3** 'Eric has done wrong, but he is also a victim.' Write a paragraph either **for** or **against** this statement.

## Chart the break-up of the family

**1** Copy the following table, then add to it to chart the break-up of the Birling family in the play so far.

| Disagreement | Quotation |
|---|---|
| Eric and Birling argue when Birling tells the story of Eva being sacked. | 'Birling: She was one of my employees and then I discharged her.<br>Eric: Is that why she committed suicide? When was this father?<br>Birling: Just keep quiet Eric and don't get excited.' |
| Sheila feels her father's action may have led to Eva Smith's unhappiness. | 'Sheila: I think it was a mean thing to do. Perhaps that spoilt everything for her.<br>Birling: Rubbish!' |

Continue to add to the table as you read through to the end of the play.

You don't understand anything. You never did.

*Eric: Act Three*

> **Learning checkpoint**
>
> Look back over the extract, then write two or three paragraphs describing and explaining your interpretation of the relationship between Eric and Mr Birling. Here are some examples to get you started:
>
> - Eric's line … suggests …
> - When Mr Birling … , it suggests that …
> - Priestley uses language to show that …
>
> **How will I know I've done this well?**
>
> ✔ Use at least one quotation from the text to support the points you make.
> ✔ Show how Priestley uses language and dramatic devices to present everything that Eric and Mr Birling say and do.
> ✔ Use accurate spelling and clear, well-punctuated sentences.

## GETTING IT INTO WRITING

In your exam, there will be a choice of two questions on *An Inspector Calls*. You will answer **one** question. The question may include a statement for you to respond to. There will be two supporting bullet points to help you address the question. One example of a question might look like this:

---

**How does Priestley present (character/situation/event/relationship/idea/etc.) in *An Inspector Calls*?** Write about:

- how the (character/situation/event/relationship/idea/etc.) is explored in the play
- how Priestley presents the (character/situation/event/relationship/idea/etc.) by the way he writes.

---

In previous units you have developed your skills to plan and write a literature essay. You have thought about:

- how to understand the task
- how to do a detailed essay plan
- how to work with quotations.

You have practised bringing these together to produce a piece of sustained writing and have had the opportunity to write under timed conditions.

Remember: in the exam you will have to write about the whole play. You will have 45 minutes to write your essay.

**1** Look at the information you have been given about question structure. Choose a **character**, situation, event, relationship or idea in the play and think about a question you would like to answer for this.

Use your work from this unit, but try to widen it by looking back at your notes and ideas from previous units.

Now plan and write your answer to this question.

✓ **Complete this assignment on Cambridge Elevate.**

## GETTING FURTHER

### The world beyond the play

**1** Look back to the notes you made in Unit 3 about Priestley's views on society. What does Priestley's examination of the conflict between the generations suggest about his wider view of society?

**2** Look at this list of objects that might be found in the Birling's house:

- Mr Birling: a painting of a racehorse in a gilt frame
- Sheila: an old and battered rocking horse
- Mrs Birling: a photo of Birling as a young man
- Eric: a boy's cricket cap that has fallen behind a dresser.

Use your knowledge of the play so far to imagine the world of the characters beyond the text.

a   Imagine why each of the objects might be significant for the named character.
b   In small groups, discuss the objects.
c   Think about the stories that might lie behind the objects and how they could be significant to the character.
d   Prepare a **monologue** spoken by the character, in which they tell the story behind the object.

**3** Prepare a dramatic reading of the extract in this unit.

- **a** In groups, decide who will read which character.
- **b** Before you start the read-through, work on your own, studying your character's words.
- **c** In each of your speeches, find two or three key words – the ones that seem most important. This will help you with **emphasis** and **expression**. It is important to understand what your character is saying and why they are saying it. If you don't understand your words, your audience won't either.
- **d** Make sure you understand your character's speeches, motivations and relationship to the other characters.
- **e** Read the extract to yourself as if you are acting it, thinking carefully about how you will say each line. You might find it helpful to practise saying your lines quietly to yourself.
- **f** Work with a partner and coach each other by going through your lines and speaking them aloud. Discuss the meaning of your words.
- **g** When you feel you are fully prepared, get together with the other actors in your group and read through the extract. Remember to make the read-through dramatic – think of it as a performance.

**4** Afterwards, discuss how your reading of the extract has helped you to understand the characters, and what they say and do.

> **Key terms**
>
> **monologue:** a long speech given by a character in a play to another character or characters.
>
> **emphasis:** the extra force given to a word or phrase when a writer wants it to make a particular impact.
>
> **expression:** the way that a word or phrase is spoken to show feeling or emotion.

# 9

## Revelations and responsibility

How does Priestley develop ideas about social responsibility?

Your progress in this unit:
- illustrate and interrogate the characters' actions in the play
- form ideas and perspectives about the theme of social responsibility
- prepare a case for the characters in a courtroom drama.

## GETTING STARTED – THE PLAY AND YOU

### Who is responsible?

Look at the following scenario.

> A teacher leaves the room. Katie tells Sam to take Sarah's phone out of her bag whilst she's not looking. Sam does so. Katie rings Sarah's phone. Sarah recognises her ringtone and hunts around the room, finding the phone in the bin. The class roars with laughter. Just as she finds it, three Year 10 students burst into the room. The door hits Sarah, who drops her phone and screams. The phone smashes into pieces on the floor. Sarah screams, 'My life is ruined! I have no phone!'

**1** Imagine you are the deputy head teacher sent to investigate. Write three paragraphs to summarise your investigation. Who do you think is responsible for what happened? Explain your reasons.

**2** In small groups, discuss recent news stories where a single person has been held responsible for something that has happened. Is it always possible (or fair) to hold one person responsible? Can or should people share responsibility when bad things happen?

## GETTING CLOSER – FOCUS ON DETAILS

### Reactions to Eva's death

Read the play from the end of the extract in Unit 8 to where Birling threatens to throw Eric out.

**1** Write a tweet (no more than 140 characters) from each **character** in this section, summarising how they feel about Eva Smith's death at this point in the play.

**2** Match these quotations with the character that speaks them.

- a 'Eric, I'm absolutely ashamed of you.'
- b 'It doesn't much matter now, of course – but was he really a police inspector?'
- c 'You're beginning to pretend now that nothing's really happened at all.'
- d 'That's comic, that is, coming from you. You're the one it makes most difference to.'
- e 'Well, I must say his manner was quite extraordinary; so – so rude – and assertive–'

**3** What do these quotations tell us about each character's reaction to Eva's death?

## 9 Revelations and responsibility

### WHAT HAPPENS NEXT?

After the Inspector has prevented the family from almost coming to blows, he sums up how they each helped to kill Eva Smith.

Birling offers money as a bribe, hoping that the Inspector will keep quiet.

Before he leaves, the Inspector lectures them about social responsibility: **'We don't live alone. We are members of one body. We are responsible for each other.'**

Birling turns on Eric, blaming him for the mess they are in. Sheila says that her father does not seem to have learnt anything. She is then struck by the thought that the Inspector might not have been a police inspector at all. However, she soon realises that it doesn't make any difference if he was or not – they still did what they did.

They unpick the Inspector's questioning, realise that he had little information and wonder if they have been tricked. Gerald comes back from his walk and tells them that he met a police officer who had never heard of Inspector Goole. Birling phones the chief constable, who confirms there is no such man on the local force.

Birling is relieved to discover that this has been a hoax, but is still angry with Sheila and Eric, whom he feels have given too much away. But Eric and Sheila still feel ashamed. Sheila says to her mother and father, **'You're just beginning to pretend all over again.'**

Eric says the fact remains that the girl is dead and they all helped to kill her. Birling threatens to throw him out of the house and Eric says he does not care whether he stays or not.

## Ideas of social responsibility

**1** Copy and complete the following table to explore the characters' attitudes to social responsibility as revealed after the Inspector leaves.

| Character | Attitude to social responsibility |
|---|---|
| Birling | not interested in change<br>only concerned about self<br>remains fixed in the belief that a man has to look after himself |
| Mrs Birling | |
| Sheila | |
| Eric | |

**2** Look closely at the Inspector's final speech:

> One Eva Smith has gone — but there are millions and millions and millions of Eva Smiths and John Smiths still left with us, with their lives, their hopes and fears, their suffering and chance of happiness, all intertwined with our lives, and what we say and do. We don't live alone. We are members of one body. We are responsible for each other.

Which of these statements do you feel best explains what the Inspector is implying?

a  We should feel sorry for all the people who are poor and unhappy like Eva Smith.
b  Eva Smith is gone but she can be replaced by all the other people like her, who are kind and thoughtful.
c  We have seen how Eva Smith has been mistreated and we should realise that we are responsible for all the people like her. We should not make these mistakes again.

**3** Why does the Inspector widen his speech to include '**millions and millions and millions of Eva Smiths and John Smiths**'? What effect does this have for an audience?

**4** The Inspector's final words are:

> And I tell you that the time will soon come when, if men will not learn that lesson, then they will be taught it in fire and blood and anguish.

a  Write a short paragraph explaining what you think he means by this.
b  What does this tell us about the message Priestley was trying to give the audience?

> We are members of one body. We are responsible for each other.
>
> *Inspector: Act Three*

# 9 Revelations and responsibility

## PUTTING DETAILS TO USE

### The theme of responsibility

We've selected this extract to help you develop your understanding of the play and so that you can have more confidence to use textual evidence in your written responses.

**Birling** […] Just remember your own position, young man. If anybody's up to the neck in this business, you are, so you'd better take some interest in it.

**Eric** I do take some interest in it. I take too much, that's my trouble.

**Sheila** It's mine too.

**Birling** Now listen, you two. If you're still feeling on edge, then the least you can do is to keep quiet. Leave this to us. I'll admit that fellow's antics rattled us a bit. But we've found him out – and all we have to do is to keep our heads. Now it's our turn.

**Sheila** Our turn to do – what?

**Mrs B.** (*sharply*) To behave sensibly, Sheila – which is more than you're doing.

**Eric** (*bursting out*) What's the use of talking about behaving sensibly. You're beginning to pretend now that nothing's really happened at all. And I can't see it like that. This girl's still dead, isn't she? Nobody's brought her to life, have they?

**Sheila** (*eagerly*) That's just what I feel, Eric. And it's what they don't seem to understand.

**Eric** Whoever that chap was, the fact remains that I did what I did. And mother did what she did. And the rest of you did what you did to her. It's still the same rotten story whether it's been told to a police inspector or to somebody else. According to you, I ought to feel a lot better—(*To* GERALD.) I stole some money, Gerald, you might as well know—(*As* BIRLING *tries to interrupt.*) I don't care, let him know. The money's not the important thing. It's what happened to the girl and what we all did to her that matters. And I still feel the same about it, and that's why I don't feel like sitting down and having a nice cosy talk.

**Sheila** And Eric's absolutely right. And it's the best thing any one of us has said tonight and it makes me feel a bit less ashamed of us. You're just beginning to pretend all over again.

**Birling** Look – for God's sake!

**Mrs B.** (*protesting*) Arthur!

**Birling** Well, my dear, they're so damned exasperating. They just won't try to understand our position or to see the difference between a lot of stuff like this coming out in private and a downright public scandal.

**Eric** (*shouting*) And I say the girl's dead and we all helped to kill her – and that's what matters—

**Birling** (*also shouting, threatening* ERIC) And I say – either stop shouting or get out. (*Glaring at him but in quiet tone.*) Some fathers I know would have kicked you out of the house anyhow by this time. So hold your tongue if you want to stay here.

**Eric** (*quietly, bitterly*) I don't give a damn now whether I stay here or not.

## GCSE English Literature for AQA: An Inspector Calls

1. **'Just remember your own position, young man'**. Write a paragraph explaining why Birling is so keen to shift the responsibility on to Eric. What does this imply about his own sense of responsibility?

2. What evidence can you find in the extract to suggest that Birling's attitudes have remained unchanged since the beginning of the play?

3. What do you think Mrs Birling means by '**behaving sensibly**'?

4. How does Eric's attitude change when the Inspector's authenticity is called into question?

5. Sheila says, '**And it's what they don't seem to understand.**' Why is her use of the word '**they**' significant?

6. Sheila says, '**And it's the best thing any one of us has said tonight**'. Write a paragraph analysing the meaning of this quotation.

7. What evidence can you find in the extract to suggest how Eric's ideas and perspectives have been changed by what has happened?

8. Find two quotations to suggest what has happened to Mrs Birling's attitudes in the course of the play.

 Find out more about themes and ideas in the play in Unit 14.

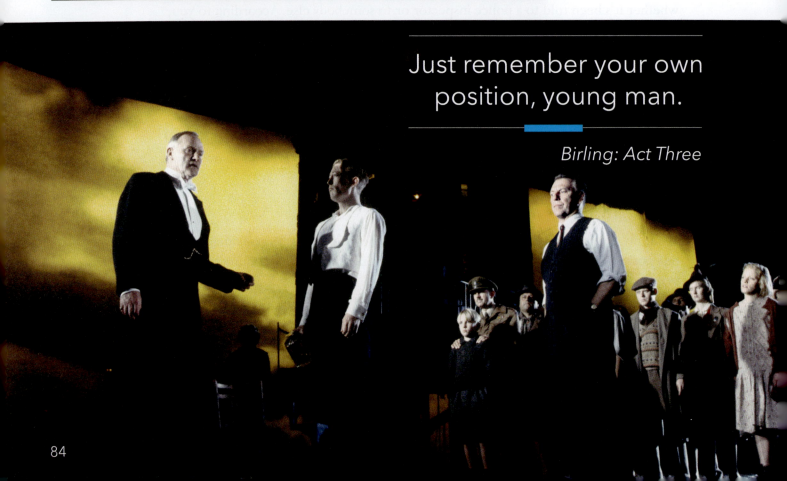

## Just remember your own position, young man.

*Birling: Act Three*

## Courtroom drama

You are going to put Priestley's characters on trial to determine their responsibility for Eva Smith's death.

By the end of the trial, you should have established:

- the ideas that Priestley explores through each character
- the effect Priestley intends each character's actions and words to have on the audience.

For each character, you will need three people:

- one to play the character
- one to play their defence lawyer
- one to play the prosecuting lawyer.

You can choose to put any (or all) of the main characters in the dock.

**Defendant:** Think hard about your character. Look at all the evidence in the text and consider whether you should show any remorse for your actions. What exactly do you think you are guilty of – if anything?

**Defence lawyer:** Work with the character in the dock (the defendant) to prepare the arguments for their defence. Your aim is to show that your client is not responsible for Eva Smith's death.

You will need to:

- think of questions that will show the defendant is not guilty
- provide evidence from the text to back up your arguments.

**Prosecuting lawyer:** The job of the prosecution is to try and prove that the defendant is responsible for the death of Eva Smith. The prosecuting lawyer should not work with the defendant or the defence lawyer. However, prosecuting lawyers might want to work alongside each other to:

- share ideas and help each other out
- prepare questions
- find evidence from the text to back up their case.

**Judge and jury:** You need to consider the arguments that each side puts forward.

### Mr Birling

**The prosecution** will find plenty of evidence to show that he lacks judgement and is 'behind the times'. They will also demonstrate that he feels no remorse for his actions unless he thinks there are consequences.

**The defence** will find evidence to show that Mr Birling thinks people should take responsibility for their own actions and that he is a responsible and successful businessman who needs to look after his company before anything else.

### Sheila

**The prosecution** can say that she complained about Eva and got her the sack for a trivial and selfish reason. She was vain.

**The defence** can argue that she was young and naïve at the start of the play. There is lots of evidence of her remorse and her intentions to change.

### Gerald

**The prosecution** can say that he used Eva as a mistress and then just dropped her. At the end of the play, he is still desperate to get himself off the hook.

**The defence** will be able to argue that he showed care and had genuine feelings for her. There is evidence of this, even from the Inspector himself.

### Mrs Birling

**The prosecution** can show she knew how desperate Eva was and refused to help her.

**The defence** will have a difficult task. They may have to argue that her actions were because of her stupidity, or believing too much in the class system and social structures of her time. They might want to refer to her charity work.

### Eric

**The prosecution** can find evidence that Eric used Eva for sex and had no regard for the consequences of his behaviour.

**The defence** can argue that he tried to help her by giving her money he had stolen from the family business. They might look at his difficult relationship with his family, and with his father in particular.

### The Inspector

**The defence** might think that he has done nothing wrong except investigate the case.

**The prosecution** can refer to the end of the play when the characters find out there was no Inspector and no suicide. They may say that the death was entirely his responsibility because he made it all up!

- Are there any arguments to counter this? He is called Inspector 'Goole' – do you think this name might be significant?
- At the end of the play the audience discovers that a girl has indeed killed herself. Do you think the Inspector being real or not has any bearing on the facts of the case?

**1** Follow these steps to conduct your trial:

- a  The judge introduces the case.
- b  The prosecution lawyer puts forward the case against Birling.
- c  The defence lawyer puts forward the defence of Birling.
- d  Birling comes into the witness box and is cross-examined.
- e  If the defence wishes, they can ask further questions of Birling.
- f  The prosecution sums up their case.
- g  The defence sums up their case.
- h  Each of the prepared cases is heard.
- i  The jury retires to discuss their verdict.
- j  The court returns and the foreman of the jury gives the verdict.

The judge needs to keep order and direct proceedings. The jury (the rest of the class) makes notes.

## GETTING IT INTO WRITING

### Writing about the theme of responsibility

**1** Work in groups of three or four. Use your evidence from the courtroom activity to discuss how Priestley explores the theme of responsibility in *An Inspector Calls*.

In the courtroom drama, you dealt with the characters as if they were real. In your discussion, remember that the characters are carefully constructed by Priestley for dramatic effect.

Discuss and make notes on the following:

- a the ways in which each character is responsible for Eva's death
- b how Priestley goes about exposing each character's responsibility
- c the role of the Inspector and his views
- d how the Inspector's views represent those of Priestley
- e the **context** of 1945 and how this might have influenced the ideas in the play
- f the structure of the play, leading to the Inspector's final speech and the characters' reactions.

**2** On your own, choose three of the points a–f and write up your notes into paragraphs.

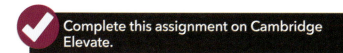
Complete this assignment on Cambridge Elevate.

## GETTING FURTHER

### Why did Priestley write this play?

**1** Do you think Priestley wrote *An Inspector Calls* to ask questions or to help us find answers? Give your reasons.

**2** If Priestley wanted to make people think about the idea of responsibility, some people say there is a problem with the ending of the play. If everyone is responsible for something that happens, can't we just say, 'Well, okay, I'm responsible, but so is everyone else.' Might this argument be an excuse for doing nothing? Explain your answer.

# 10

## Ideas and attitudes

**What do the characters learn from the Inspector's visit?**

---

Your progress in this unit:
- reflect on the play as a whole and explore the journeys of the different characters
- interrogate the perspectives that the characters have developed
- consider how Priestley has asked the audience to think beyond the play and into their own world.

### GETTING STARTED – THE PLAY AND YOU

### What have you learnt?

**1** Which of the **characters** in the play do you think is most like you in the way they think and behave? Why?

**2** A play has only worked for an audience if they feel the experience of watching it (or studying it) has been worthwhile. What have you learnt from the Inspector's visit?

**3** Imagine you are the Inspector. What would you be thinking if you could see the reaction of the characters after you have left? Work in small groups to rank the following statements according to how well they sum up the Inspector's feelings.

a Everyone seems to have learnt the error of their ways.
b This is just the kind of reaction I wanted – a good family row.
c I've failed. I still haven't found out who killed Eva Smith.
d They were supposed to think about their responsibility but they are still arguing.
e It's about the argument and the discussion, not about finding the right answer – so my visit has been a success.

### GETTING CLOSER – FOCUS ON DETAILS

### Language and characterisation

Look at the summary, then read from the end of the extract in Unit 9 to the end of the play.

**1** Look at how Priestley uses language in this section of the play to show us the response of each character after the Inspector leaves. Find a quotation for each character that sums up their feelings and attitude. Use a copy of the following table to record your answers. An example has been done to start you off.

| Character | Their feelings and attitude | Quotation |
|---|---|---|
| Birling | He thinks it was a hoax and dismisses the whole experience as a joke. | 'You'll have a good laugh over it yet.' |
| | | |

10 Ideas and attitudes

## WHAT HAPPENS NEXT?

Mr and Mrs Birling are satisfied that the Inspector was a fraud. Gerald points out they only have the Inspector's word that it was the same girl he showed them all in the photographs – none of them saw it at the same time.

Eric says it doesn't matter because the girl he knew is dead, but Gerald asks how they know that any girl killed herself today. He rings the Infirmary and finds out that no girl has died there that night.

Birling and Gerald are delighted. Birling laughs and admits the Inspector did give him a bit of a scare.

Sheila is still troubled by the Inspector's words and won't be persuaded. Gerald tries to calm her down by telling her everything is all right now. He asks her about the ring but she says she needs time to think.

At that moment, the phone rings and Birling answers it. He comes off the phone. Panic-stricken, he explains that a girl has just died in the Infirmary and a police inspector is on his way to ask them some questions …

## PUTTING DETAILS TO USE

### What the characters learn

We've selected this extract to help you develop your understanding of the play and so that you can have more confidence to use textual evidence in your written responses.

| | |
|---|---|
| **Birling** | (*giving him a drink*) Yes, he didn't keep you on the run as he did the rest of us. I'll admit now he gave me a bit of a scare at the time. But I'd a special reason for not wanting any public scandal just now. (*Has his drink now, and raises his glass.*) Well, here's to us. Come on, Sheila, don't look like that. All over now. |
| **Sheila** | The worst part is. But you're forgetting one thing I still can't forget. Everything we said had happened really had happened. If it didn't end tragically, then that's lucky for us. But it might have done. |
| **Birling** | (*jovially*) But the whole thing's different now. Come, come, you can see that, can't you? (*Imitating* INSPECTOR *in his final speech.*) You all helped to kill her. (*Pointing at* SHEILA *and* ERIC, *and laughing.*) And I wish you could have seen the look on your faces when he said that. |
| | SHEILA *moves towards door.* |
| | Going to bed, young woman? |
| **Sheila** | (*tensely*) I want to get out of this. It frightens me the way you talk. |
| **Birling** | (*heartily*) Nonsense! You'll have a good laugh over it yet. Look, you'd better ask Gerald for that ring you gave back to him, hadn't you? Then you'll feel better. |
| **Sheila** | (*passionately*) You're pretending everything's just as it was before. |
| **Eric** | I'm not! |
| **Sheila** | No, but these others are. |
| **Birling** | Well, isn't it? We've been had, that's all. |
| **Sheila** | So nothing really happened. So there's nothing to be sorry for, nothing to learn. We can all go on behaving just as we did. |
| **Mrs B.** | Well, why shouldn't we? |
| **Sheila** | I tell you – whoever that Inspector was, it was anything but a joke. You knew it then. You began to learn something. And now you've stopped. You're ready to go on in the same old way. |
| **Birling** | (*amused*) And you're not, eh? |
| **Sheila** | No, because I remember what he said, how he looked, and what he made me feel. Fire and blood and anguish. And it frightens me the way you talk, and I can't listen to any more of it. |
| **Eric** | And I agree with Sheila. It frightens me too. |
| **Birling** | Well, go to bed then, and don't stand there being hysterical. |

**10 Ideas and attitudes**

| | |
|---|---|
| **Mrs B.** | They're over-tired. In the morning they'll be as amused as we are. |
| **Gerald** | Everything's all right now, Sheila. (*Holds up the ring.*) What about this ring? |
| **Sheila** | No, not yet. It's too soon. I must think. |
| **Birling** | (*pointing to* ERIC *and* SHEILA) Now look at the pair of them – the famous younger generation who know it all. And they can't even take a joke— |

*The telephone rings sharply. There is a moment's complete silence.* BIRLING *goes to answer it.*

Yes? … Mr Birling speaking … What? – here—

*But obviously the other person has rung off. He puts the telephone down slowly and looks in a panic-stricken fashion at the others.*

**Birling** That was the police. A girl has just died – on her way to the Infirmary – after swallowing some disinfectant. And a police inspector is on his way here – to ask some – questions—

*As they stare guiltily and dumbfounded, the curtain falls.*

---

**1** Find two quotations that suggest that Birling has not been changed by the events of the last hour.

**2** '**Going to bed, young woman?**' What are Birling's reasons for calling Sheila '**young woman**'? Explain what this suggests about their relationship.

**3** '**And I must say, Gerald, you've argued this very cleverly, and I'm most grateful.**' What do you think this quotation reveals about Mrs Birling's attitude to change? Discuss this in pairs or small groups.

 Find out more about character and characterisation in the play in Unit 13.

That was the police.
A girl has just died …

*Birling: Act Three*

4. Why do you think Mrs Birling finds it so difficult to accept that what she did was wrong?

5. Look at the Birlings' last words to their children. What do these words tell the audience about what they have learnt from the Inspector's visit?

6. Gerald only says one line in this extract.

   a   What does this line suggest about the effect the Inspector's visit has had on him?
   b   Write a short **monologue** from Gerald's point of view in which he expresses his feelings at the end of the play.

7. Sheila says she wants to '**get out of this**'.

   a   What does this line reveal about the thoughts that are going through her mind?
   b   Write a paragraph from Sheila's point of view, in which she expresses her feelings about her parents.

8. Sheila uses the words '**fire and blood and anguish**'.

   a   Why do you think Priestley has given her these words?
   b   What does this suggest about the way she will develop when the play has finished?

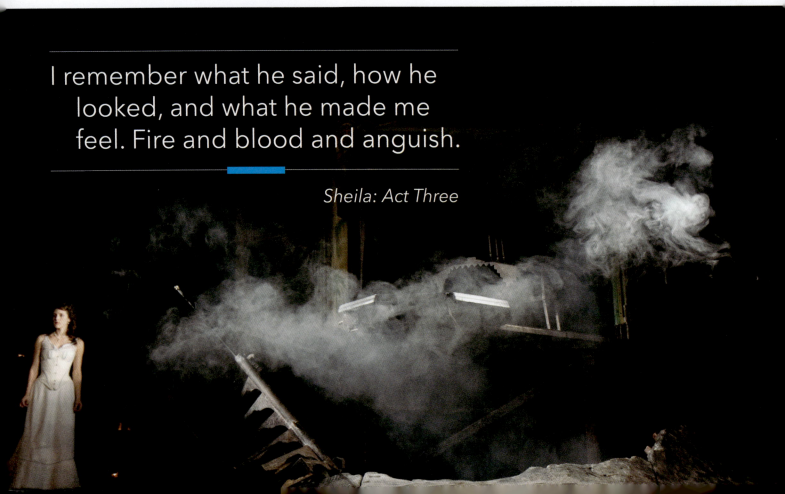

I remember what he said, how he looked, and what he made me feel. Fire and blood and anguish.

*Sheila: Act Three*

# 10 Ideas and attitudes

## The play and the audience

**1** Discuss the following questions in small groups.

  **a** Do you think the Birling family will change after their visit from the Inspector?

  **b** If the play is representative of society, in your opinion whose attitude will win: that of Sheila and Eric or that of Mr and Mrs Birling?

**2** Discuss the following questions in small groups.

  **a** What do you think Priestley's own ideas and perspectives were?

  **b** Has Priestley allowed his own opinions to intrude too much into the drama?

  **c** Does he make his ideas and perspectives too obvious through his characters?

**3** Some people believe that the ending of the play is too clever. Up to now, everything in the play has seemed very realistic, especially the characters, but the ending adds an almost supernatural element. Do you agree that the ending does not 'fit' with the rest of the play? Give reasons for your answer.

**4** Write a short paragraph about the ending of the play, its dramatic impact, and the effect that Priestley intended this to have on the audience.

### Learning checkpoint

Write a paragraph for each of the characters, summarising what you feel they have learnt from the Inspector's visit. Use the notes that you have made for the activities in this unit so far as a starting point for your writing. Make sure that you use supporting details and quotations from the text to support any comments that you make about the characters.

**How will I know I've done this well?**

When you have finished writing, check back over your answer to make sure you have:

- ✔ included your own interpretations about the characters
- ✔ supported your points by referring to at least one quotation in the text for each of the characters
- ✔ explored the techniques Priestley has used in his **characterisation**
- ✔ written in well-organised paragraphs
- ✔ used accurate spelling and clear, well-punctuated sentences.

# GETTING IT INTO WRITING

## Writing about attitude

**1** Choose two characters in the extract and explain how one has changed and one has not changed. Use details of what they say in the extract and what they said earlier, as well as their relationship with other characters.

You might find it helpful to look back over the essay-writing skills you have learnt from previous units. Remember: in examination questions, you will be expected to refer to the **whole play**.

**Ideas to consider**

You could use some of the following prompts to get you thinking about your answer. Remember, none of them is supported by evidence. You will need to find relevant details and quotations in the text to support any points you make, and use them in an appropriate way.

- how Priestley shows the response to the Inspector's visit to be divided between the older and younger generation
- the ways in which Birling remains unchanged from his self-centred views and misplaced optimism
- how Mrs Birling remains the **stereotype** of an upper middle-class woman at the beginning of the 20th century
- how Gerald's life is thrown into uncertainty by Sheila's refusal to accept the engagement ring and what wider comment Priestley might be making about class
- how Priestley uses Sheila and Eric to represent the hope for change that the next generation will bring
- the journey that Sheila's character makes from a wealthy young girl who seems fascinated by material objects to an independent woman who challenges the ideas of her parent's generation

 Complete this assignment on Cambridge Elevate.

## GETTING FURTHER

### More about the theme of responsibility

The following novels all deal with the theme of responsibility, although they do so in very different ways. They were all written at different times.

- In *Great Expectations* (1861), by Charles Dickens, Pip's life is thrown into confusion when a secret benefactor pays for him to go to London and be educated to become a gentleman. This dream of wealth and fortune turns into a nightmare. But who is responsible?
- The American novel *Of Mice and Men* (1937) by John Steinbeck is the story of two farm workers. George looks after Lennie, but at the end of the novel he has to take responsibility for a dreadful action. How do we judge him for his actions?
- In Mary Shelley's *Frankenstein* (1818), Dr Frankenstein wants to recreate life and makes a creature from the body parts of dead people. The creature he creates is unhappy and confused. What responsibility does science have for the monsters it creates?

**1** How might the times when these novels were written have influenced the ideas presented in them?

**2** All three of these novels have been adapted as successful plays for the theatre and as films. You might find it interesting to watch one or more of these films or recordings of theatre performances, considering the theme of responsibility in each story.

# 11

## Plot and structure

How does Priestley take his audience on a journey of discovery?

---

Your progress in this unit:
- understand and explain the structure of the plot
- interpret the theatricality and dramatic impact of the play
- explore how the play develops
- write about plot and structure.

## THE PLOT OF *AN INSPECTOR CALLS*

*An Inspector Calls* is set in 1912, in the dining room of the Birlings' house. The play is divided into three acts, in which the Inspector investigates the '**chain of events**' that led to the suicide of a young woman, Eva Smith. He investigates the Birling family with '**one line of enquiry at a time**', in which he reveals their responsibility in the events that led to Eva's death. The play leaves the audience asking several questions:

- Who is the young woman?
- Who is the Inspector?
- Who is responsible?

## THEATRICAL AND DRAMATIC STRUCTURE

In *An Inspector Calls*, Priestley draws on forms of theatre such as naturalism, the drawing-room drama (detective stories or 'whodunnits') and the **well-made play**. The play follows a classic three-act structure, which reflects the three unities of Greek tragedy (unity of time, place and action).

### Naturalism

Naturalism is a form of theatre in which an audience sees real **characters** in a natural setting. You forget that you are watching a play and that you are being told a story. It is as if you are spying on these people as they go about their everyday lives. Naturalism is sometimes described as 'fourth wall drama' because it is as if you are looking into a room where the fourth wall has been removed. As an audience you observe what is happening.

Naturalism became a very important form of theatre towards the end of the 19th century and remained popular into the 20th century. However, some playwrights disliked the ideas of naturalism. Berthold Brecht believed that in this kind of performance an audience became so engrossed in the events on stage that they stopped thinking. He said that 'they hung their brains up with their hats and coats in the cloakroom'.

### The drawing-room drama and detective stories

Drawing-room drama comprised a short play that could be performed in the room of a Victorian middle-class home. Naturalism suited this kind of drama because the furniture could be used as the set. Detective stories or 'whodunnits' were an ideal genre for the drawing-room drama. The interest for the audience was in trying to work out which of the characters was guilty of the crime. Priestley's audience would have been familiar with the conventions of this form.

## The well-made play and the three classic unities

*An Inspector Calls* is a well-made play that progresses from ignorance to knowledge, following a classic three-act structure. Priestley uses the unities of time, place and action, first thought of by the Greek philosopher Aristotle. However he does not stick to them throughout – in fact he often subverts the rules and seems to enjoy doing so.

### Unity of time
Unity of time means that the characters are living in real time. We watch them for 90 minutes of their lives talking in their dining room. However:

- they tell stories about events that took place over the last year
- the play ends with a phone call, suggesting that the Inspector has travelled through time at the beginning.

*An Inspector Calls* is known as one of Priestley's 'time' plays, reflecting some of the 'time theories' of the period in which he was writing. At the end of the play Priestley plays with time, exploring the relationship between past, present and future.

### Unity of place
Priestley sets the play in a constant place throughout – the dining room. He uses the characters to tell different stories set in different places, such as Milwards and the Palace theatre bar. This makes the play dramatically interesting.

### Unity of action
Unity of action means that the action of the play should be based around one event. However, in *An Inspector Calls* we hear about one event – the death of Eva Smith – from lots of different points of view. Think about the different stories of Eva Smith and how the Inspector takes '**one line of enquiry at a time**', showing each individual a photo. What might Priestley be asking the audience to consider?

 Find out about the unities of time, place and action on Cambridge Elevate.

### Cyclical structure

The play begins and ends in the same way – a police inspector is on his way to the Birlings' house following the death of a young woman. Why do you think Priestley has chosen this cyclical structure?

 **Key terms**

**well-made play:** a genre of play that follows a carefully constructed plot, often based on a secret that is revealed at the climax.

GCSE English Literature for AQA: An Inspector Calls

One line of enquiry at a time.

*Inspector: Act One*

## THE THREE-ACT STRUCTURE

Look at the diagram and outline for the classic three-act structure of a play. This has been used since the days of classical Greek theatre and is still widely used today – you may recognise it, as almost all popular films follow this structure.

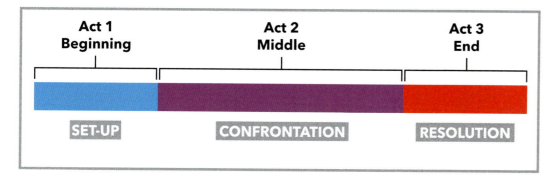

### Act 1: The beginning – the set-up

- A problem for the characters and/or the audience is set up.
- The characters are established. The main character is called the protagonist. The character against them is called the antagonist.
- The normal life of the characters is established, alongside the setting. You get to find out a bit about them. There is a hint at some of the conflicts or disagreements between them.
- Some major ideas are introduced and a mood is established. The genre is established, and the problem for the story or the narrative enigma is set up.
- The plot thickens and the 'inciting incident' is introduced. The story turns in a new direction and becomes more complicated, raising the stakes and setting up what Act 2 is going to be about.

### Act 2: The middle – the confrontation

- The story becomes more dramatic as the characters and the audience struggle to find a solution to the problem. Further complications to finding the solution are used to make the story more interesting. There are twists and turns of the plot. These are called turning points.
- A turning point is reached as the main character reaches a dramatic climax.
- A possible solution is presented. The act ends on a cliff-hanger.

### Act 3: The end – the resolution

- The protagonist achieves their mission. The conflict or problem is resolved and the final crisis (or 'rising action') plays out.
- The denouement takes place and the characters come down from the drama – this is sometimes called the 'falling action'. The characters (and the audience) have learnt something. Their lives have been changed.
- Narrative closure takes place as the story ends. Sometimes an unexpected ending, or twist, is added to surprise the audience.

> **Key terms**
>
> **denouement:** the final part of a play, when all the strands of the plot are drawn together and resolved.

# GCSE English Literature for AQA: An Inspector Calls

## DEVELOP AND REVISE

### Three acts

The timeline of the three-act structure could be represented like this:

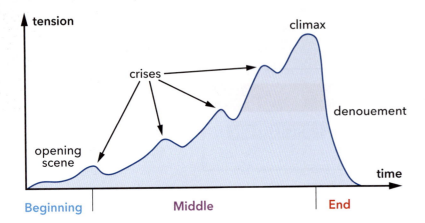

1. Copy the timeline onto a large piece of paper. Pick out the elements of a three-act play for *An Inspector Calls* and write them in the appropriate place.

2. Write a tweet (140 characters) summarising what happens in each act of the play's three acts.

### Interpret the action

1. Work in groups of three. Stand facing each other. A starts to tell the story of *An Inspector Calls*. When A claps their hands, B explains what Priestley is doing in this part of the play and the importance of the words or events described. When B has finished, they take up the story. When B claps their hands, C explains the importance of this point in the play, and so on until you reach the end of the play. If one of you gets stuck, call 'share' and share ideas.

   As you do this, consider:

   a   how Priestley uses the dramatic action of the play – for example the way he sets the scene at the opening of the play, makes the end of each act a cliff-hanger and ends the play with a circular action

   b   how Priestley uses the role of the Inspector to highlight the role each character played in the death of Eva Smith

   c   how Priestley uses characters and **characterisation** to represent ideas – for example how Mr and Mrs Birling (the older generation) and Gerald (close to the values of Mr Birling) do not change at the end of the play, and the way that Sheila and Eric (the younger generation) develop and change by the end of the play.

# 12

## Context and setting

How does Priestley bring the characters and the action alive?

Your progress in this unit:
- understand and explore the context and setting of *An Inspector Calls*
- understand how audiences would have watched and understood the play in Priestley's time
- explore the ways in which the action can be presented on stage.

### THE CONTEXT AND SETTING OF THE PLAY

Priestley wrote *An Inspector Calls* in the winter of 1944 and the spring of 1945. However, he set the play in 1912 because of the different attitudes and ideas that were common earlier in the century. Capitalism was at its height, and society was characterised by strict class divisions. Women were campaigning for the right to vote and the tensions that led to the First World War and later the Russian Revolution were already simmering.

#### The audience of 1946

The audience that watched *An Inspector Calls* in London in 1946 may have lived through two world wars and brought that perspective to the play. They would have appreciated Priestley's use of **dramatic irony** in Birling's confidence that there will be no war, that the *Titanic* is unsinkable, and that the wealth of a capitalist society will continue. The audience of 1946 would have arrived at the theatre through a bomb-damaged London and know the truth of events. This use of dramatic irony would make it clear to an audience that they cannot trust the judgement of this **character**.

*An Inspector Calls* is often called a 'play of contrasts'. Certainly the audience in 1946 would have been aware of the contrasts right from the start. How might audiences in other **contexts** of time and place respond to the play? How do **you** respond to the play?

### THE SETTING OF THE PLAY

In *An Inspector Calls*, an important understanding of **setting** and context is through what you see and hear on the stage in performance. Setting is really the world in which the play takes place, but this can expand into other 'worlds':

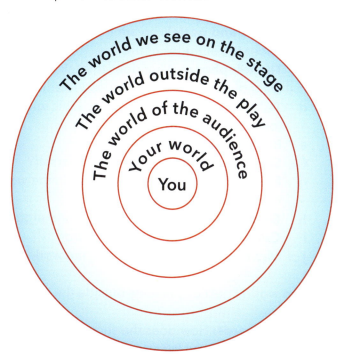

101

## DEVELOP AND REVISE

### Picturing *An Inspector Calls*

**1** Look on the internet to find photographs of different productions of *An Inspector Calls* at around the point in the play when the Inspector arrives. Choose the production that you find the most interesting. List five things you notice from the photo, such as the type of furniture, the props, the costumes or the lighting. Consider these questions:

  a   How can you tell which period of time the production is set in?
  b   What do the contents of the room tell you about the Birling family?
  c   What atmosphere is created by the design?

**2** In groups, compare your findings. Look back at the opening stage directions. Discuss the differences and similarities between the productions and how they might affect an audience.

### The worlds of the play

Use your work from earlier units to gather answers to the questions about the worlds of the play.

**1** The world Priestley presents on the stage:

  a   **Substantial and heavy furniture:** What does this tell you about the family's background?
  b   **Cigars and port:** Who are these likely to be for? What does this tell you about the attitudes of the day?
  c   **The telephone:** What does this tell you about the Birling's attitude to technology? How will it be used later in the play?
  d   **Tails and white ties:** What does this tell you about the family's attitude towards the occasion?
  e   **Birling is portentous:** Why?
  f   **Sheila:** Why is she pleased with herself?
  g   **Birling:** How does he see himself in the world? What kind of person does he represent to an audience?
  h   **Eric:** What is his attitude to the world around him?
  i   **Gerald:** How do others see his world?
  j   **Mrs Birling:** Is she happy with the world she finds herself in?

**2** The world Priestley presents outside the dining room:

  a   **Milwards:** How does the shop treat its assistants?
  b   **The Infirmary:** What does the name suggest?
  c   **The factory:** How are the workers treated?
  d   **The Palace bar:** What attitudes to sex are represented here?

> The INSPECTOR *interposes himself between them and the photograph*
>
> *Stage direction: Act One*

**3** The wider world outside the play (which the 1946 audience would be aware of):

   **a**  **The impending First World War:** What does the audience know about this that the characters don't?

   **b**  **The *Titanic*:** Birling is very proud of this – what does this suggest?

   **c**  **The miners' strike:** Why does Priestley refer to this?

**4** The world of the audience:

   **a**  **The Second World War had just ended:** What would the audience be thinking about the world?

   **b**  **In 1945–46, the new government is promising new ideas:** Is it a pessimistic or optimistic play for this time? Why?

   **c**  **The world of the audience today:** How does the play speak to you?

**5** Your world:

   **a**  What parallels are there between the play and today's world?

   **b**  What does the play have to say about your world?

   **c**  Does it challenge your attitudes?

**6** **You:** What does the play have to say about you?

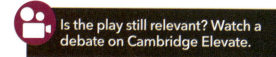

Is the play still relevant? Watch a debate on Cambridge Elevate.

# 13

## Character and characterisation

How does Priestley create such dramatic characters?

Your progress in this unit:
- understand and explore the characters in the play
- interpret how the characters represent ideas and attitudes
- explore the ways in which Priestley presents these characters
- analyse the changes in certain characters as the play progresses
- write about character and characterisation.

## THE CHARACTERS IN THE PLAY

### Arthur Birling

Mr Birling is the father of Sheila and Eric. He is married to Sybil (Mrs Birling). When we first meet Birling he is a successful businessman who is head of a well-to-do Edwardian family. He has been an alderman in the community and is now a magistrate. He believes that he will soon be given a knighthood.

He is optimistic about the future and excited by technological advances. He does not know that the *Titanic* will sink on its maiden voyage and that Europe will soon be plunged into the First World War.

During the course of the play, his self-confidence and ideas about society are exposed. He remains bullish, refusing to question his own actions.

Birling represents the establishment and he wants to keep things the way they are.

### Sybil Birling

Mrs Birling is married to Birling and is the mother of Sheila and Eric. Mrs Birling is a traditional wife of a wealthy man of this era. She is not involved in the running of the family business. She does not challenge either her husband's attitudes or the attitudes of the day. Nor does she challenge gender **stereotypes** – she expects her daughter to marry and be a dutiful wife to Gerald.

She is very judgemental and critical of people. Like Birling, the basis for her judgements is revealed to be inadequate. Her cold language, her detachment from her children and her lack of emotional warmth all suggest that she is unfulfilled and perhaps bitter, but she will never say this directly. In the play, her role as an upright member of the community is challenged and she is exposed as cruel.

### Sheila Birling

Sheila is the daughter of Arthur and Sybil Birling. She is sister to Eric and is engaged to Gerald. The play begins at her engagement party, where we are presented with a bright, pretty young girl who is happy to marry Gerald – much to her parents' approval. She has been favoured by them and is spoilt. Although she is articulate, she is more interested in clothes and jewellery than social questions, and she has no ambition other than marriage to Gerald.

During the play, her intelligence is awakened. She is the **character** who grasps what the Inspector is doing and quickly understands her own part in the death of Eva Smith. By the end of the play, she sees her parents and her place in society in a very different way. The journey that Sheila makes is the one that Priestley hopes his audience will follow.

## Eric Birling

Eric is the son of Arthur and Sybil Birling, and brother to Sheila. Eric has been a disappointment to his parents. In the play, he quarrels constantly with his father and has a drinking problem. He seems to live in the shadow of his brighter and more articulate sister. By the end of the play, he – like Sheila – shows a willingness to change, but his journey is a difficult one.

## Gerald Croft

Gerald is engaged to Sheila. He is a young aristocrat – he seems charming and is well liked by Mr and Mrs Birling. However, there is no sign of his parents at the engagement party and it is possible that they are not best pleased with the marriage plans. Gerald is not what he first seems. He has deceived Sheila and is confused by her change in the play. Crucially, although he is a member of the younger generation, he seems to want to keep the world just as it is.

## Inspector Goole

The Inspector is an enigmatic character – we never really get to know anything about his background. He is there to ask questions. He has great skill in getting people to talk. His role is to stir things up and get the characters to fall into argument. Above all, he pushes them to think about their own actions. By the end of the play, we know even less about him than we thought we did at the start.

## Edna

Edna is the maid of the Birling's household. She has only a few lines. The family see themselves as superior to her. Through Edna we can see how divided society was at this time. Even though she lives with them, the family do not consider it appropriate for her to share in Sheila's engagement celebrations.

## Eva Smith

Eva is a young woman in her early twenties. We never see her on stage but she is central to the plot. The play is concerned with uncovering her story and we discover much about her as the action unfolds. She has been badly treated by all the other characters, and has taken her own life. The question that drives the whole play forward is 'Who is responsible for her death?'

GCSE English Literature for AQA: An Inspector Calls

## DEVELOP AND REVISE

### Character tennis

**1** Work in groups of four.

**A** names a character from the play.
**B** comments on the ideas Priestley gives the character.
**C** comments on how the character changes from the beginning to the end of the play.
**D** says what they think about the character.

When you have finished, swap so A becomes B, B becomes C, C becomes D and D becomes A. Continue until you have commented on all the characters.

### Character profiles

**1** Write a list or draw a spider diagram to show how Priestley presents and uses each of the main characters of the play.

**2** How does Priestley present Eric?

    **a** Find three **turning points** in the development of Eric's character.
    **b** Find three quotations that are significant in the **characterisation** of Eric.
    **c** What are the flaws in Eric's character?

**3** How does Priestley present Mrs Birling?

    **a** Explain the way that Mrs Birling refuses to learn from her journey.
    **b** Explain her relationship with her children. Give three examples from the text.
    **c** Find three quotations that are significant in the characterisation of Mrs Birling.
    **d** How does Mrs Birling represent the traditional pre-war stereotype of women?

**4** How does Priestley present Birling?

    **a** In what ways does Birling consider himself successful at the beginning of the play?
    **b** What is his relationship like with each of his children?
    **c** Why is Birling so impressed with Gerald?

**5** How does Priestley present the Inspector?

    **a** 'A very important character, who we never get to know.' Write three bullet points that summarise how Priestley keeps the Inspector distant.
    **b** Write a paragraph that explores the idea that the Inspector might not exist at all.

## 13 Character and characterisation

**6** How does Priestley present Gerald?

  **a** 'Gerald is a charming, wealthy liar.' Write a paragraph that interrogates this statement.
  **b** Find three quotations that are significant in the characterisation of Gerald.
  **c** How does Gerald see his relationship with Sheila at the end of the play?

**7** How does Priestley present Sheila?

  **a** How does Sheila's character develop in the play?
  **b** Find three quotations that are significant in the characterisation of Sheila.
  **c** Sheila's character is a very different portrayal of a women to the character of Mrs Birling. Create a table to show the differences.

**8** Edna is the only representative of the working class that we see on stage. Write a paragraph analysing her presence in the play.

**9** Although we never see Eva Smith, she is an important character in the play. Write a paragraph exploring how Priestley uses her as a dramatic device.

Mother – stop – stop!

*Sheila: Act 2*

# 14

## Themes and ideas

**What are the big ideas that dominate *An Inspector Calls*?**

Your progress in this unit:
- understand and explore the major ideas in the play
- interpret how these themes are communicated to an audience
- explore different interpretations of and perspectives on the play
- research and write about themes in the play.

As you study the play, think about:

- how each character is involved in Eva's death
- how Birling sees his responsibility to the workers in his factory
- how Gerald sees his responsibility to tell the truth
- your own social responsibility.

### WHAT IS THE MESSAGE OF *AN INSPECTOR CALLS*?

*An Inspector Calls* deals with some big ideas, which Priestley explores from different perspectives. He did not write his play simply as an entertainment – as a writer he had things he wanted to say. These are some of the ideas that he returns to throughout the play.

### Responsibility and duty

Each **character** has to confront their share of the responsibility for Eva Smith's suicide. The action revolves around the Inspector's investigation and he reveals that all the characters have some involvement. Through the characters, Priestley asks the audience to think about their responsibility for each other and this becomes a message of the play – that we all have a collective social responsibility.

### The generations

Mr and Mrs Birling represent the older generation, whereas Sheila, Eric and Gerald are from the younger generation. The older generation want to keep things the way they are. Eric and Sheila are finally opened up to the possibility of change.

As you study the play, think about:

- why it is in Birling's interest to keep things the way they are
- Gerald's resistance to change
- whether the play looks to the future with optimism or pessimism.

### Appearance and reality

Events and characters in the play often turn out to be different from the way they first appear. The play opens in the dining room of a wealthy and successful family on the happy event of their daughter's engagement. Everything seems to be comfortable and optimistic, but the reality turns out to be very different.

As you study the play, think about:

- the ways in which ways Gerald is different from the man he appears to be
- the difference between the outward appearance of the Birlings and the reality.

## Gender

The play is set in a male-dominated world. Birling and the men are seen to benefit from this, whereas women such as Eva Smith find it hinders their progress. Even Sheila finds that she is constrained and denied the opportunity to fulfil her potential.

As you study the play, think about:

- the double standards that Gerald and Eric have towards sex
- Mrs Birling's attitude to gender roles
- how Sheila moves towards independence.

## Social class and establishment

It is 1912 and there is a rigid class system – everybody is expected to know their place. The Birlings are wealthy factory owners and are part of the upper middle class. Birling has achieved success, making money by being a part of the establishment. He has a vested interest in keeping things the way they are.

As you study the play, think about:

- how Edna is treated by the other characters
- how economic circumstance has driven Eva to despair
- whether it is fair for the wealthy to control the lives of the poor for their own profit.

## Lies and secrecy

Through his skilful questioning, the Inspector exposes lies and secrecy. Pay close attention to the ways that the characters keep the truth from one another.

As you study the play, watch out for:

- the lies Eric has told to his parents
- Birling's attempt to bribe and corrupt
- the secrets that Gerald keeps from Sheila
- the Inspector's deception – which secrets does he keep from the characters and from the audience?

# DEVELOP AND REVISE

## A lecture about responsibility

**1** Work in pairs: **A** and **B**. **A** is going to give **B** a one-minute lecture about the theme of responsibility in *An Inspector Calls*. Each point made must be supported by a quotation from the text.

Before you start, prepare by considering how Priestley presents ideas about responsibility.

- Everyone is part of one society.
- Each member of the family has a different attitude to Eva Smith's death and their responsibility.
- The words 'responsible' and 'responsibility' are used many times in the play.
- Birling believes his dismissal of Eva had nothing to do with her suicide.
- Mrs Birling believes her charity should not provide for the baby but the father should. Of course, her belief is later shaken when she finds the father is her own son.
- **Responsibility**
- Eric sees Eva as an opportunity for casual sex, but he realises his responsibility as the play progresses.
- Even though Gerald appears to have some genuine feelings for Eva, he is keen to shake off responsibility by proving the Inspector is a fake.
- Sheila is the character whose attitude and enlightenment changes the most.
- The Inspector says 'each of you helped to kill her'. His final speech widens the responsibility to suggest that even the audience might be responsible.
- The Inspector says that 'one Eva Smith has gone, but there are millions and millions and millions of Eva Smiths and John Smiths still left with us, with their lives, their hopes and fears, their suffering and chance of happiness, all intertwined with our lives, and what we think and say and do.'

 Watch a lecture about responsibility on Cambridge Elevate.

## 14 Themes and ideas

### A lecture about social class and establishment

**1** Work in the same pairs. This time **B** should choose to give a lecture on either social class or gender. Each point must include quotations from the text to support the points made.

Before you start, prepare by considering how Priestley presents ideas about social class and gender:

**Social class:**
- The play is set in the household of the Birlings – an upper middle-class family. The suggestion is that they are upwardly mobile and Birling is a self-made man.
- Mrs Birling has married beneath herself.
- Gerald Croft has aristocratic parents. Interestingly, they have chosen not to be at the engagement celebration, suggesting that they may disapprove of his choice of wife.
- Edna is the only working-class character seen by the audience in the play.
- However it is Eva Smith, a working-class girl, we get to know most about.
- Birling is soon to be knighted and accepted as a member of the upper class; he sees Eva as cheap labour.
- At the start of the play, Sheila spends her father's money in expensive shops; she sees Eva as someone she can get angry with.
- Gerald is prepared to marry Sheila, despite her lower social position, yet he sees Eva as a mistress who can be discarded at will.
- Eric faces his issues about his background by getting drunk. He sees Eva as an opportunity for casual sex.
- Mrs Birling sees herself as superior and enjoys her power over people like Eva by refusing them charity.
- The play shows us that the upper classes are unaware that the easy lives they lead rely on the hard work of the working class. The vast majority of the audience would be from the middle and upper classes.

**Gender:**
- Sheila is a rather naïve and possibly silly girl; she is impressed by a ring and is happy to go along with a marriage to a man she does not really know. Yet as the play progresses she learns and matures. She is introduced to the realities of life.
- Mrs Birling is a woman who has found wealth and stability in the class system. She has an interest in keeping things the way they are. Early on in the play she tries to control Sheila. She is pompous and refuses to accept the need for change and is exposed as being foolish.
- Because Eva Smith is a woman, she is in a worse position than a working-class man would be at the time. Her only chance for income is a job or finding a husband. This is why she is so reliant on Gerald and Eric.
- Priestley decides to write his play around the death of a young working-class woman rather than the death of a young working-class man.

## A themes decoration

**1** Using the themes in the play, create a 'themes' decoration for your classroom:

- responsibility
- the older and younger generations
- appearance and reality
- social class and establishment
- gender stereotype
- lies and secrecy.

a  Divide into groups. Each group takes one of the themes. Find 8–10 quotations from the play that show how Priestley presents and explores your chosen theme.

b  Write out your theme on a large piece of paper and surround it with the evidence you have found for how Priestley develops it throughout the play.

c  When you have finished, put all the groups' themes together as a wall display.

## A themes grid

**1** Create a grid to record how Priestley introduces and develops different themes throughout the play. For the different themes:

a  show how Priestley presents the themes through the action and the characters
b  refer to the text to support your choices
c  give your own comment or interpretation.

You could support the theme of appearance and reality, for example, with a quotation from Gerald telling the story of 'saving' Eva from the Palace bar ('**The girl … gave me a glance that was nothing less than a cry for help**') and the interpretation that he is portraying himself as a hero.

Each of you helped to kill her.

*Inspector: Act Three*

# 15 Language

Why do the language and actions in the play carry such impact?

Your progress in this unit:
- analyse and explore language across the whole play
- explore and interpret links between character and language
- write about Priestley's use of language.

## LANGUAGE IN PRIESTLEY'S WORLD

*An Inspector Calls* is a naturalistic play, which means that the language of the **characters** is written to sound like ordinary speech. Unlike Shakespeare, for example, Priestley does not write in verse, and his vocabulary and grammar are not very different from modern usage.

### Language and characterisation

Priestley shows great language skills in making his characters believable. He makes their speech distinctive and personal in order to convey their **mood** (something that changes) and **manner** (something that is part of their personality). This is all part of the craft of **characterisation**. Some people say that 'we are what we eat'; writers of plays and novels build their work on the assumption that we are what we speak – our language is the sound of our identity. For example Birling's language conveys an impression of his manner as confident, opinionated and rather patronising. Priestley conveys these qualities by making his speech full of instructions, assertions and advice to young people who do not have his experience and wisdom. His speech is full of derogatory terms such as '**cranks**', assertions such as '**there will be no war**' and instructions and advice to others such as '**I know**' and '**listen to me**'.

Mrs Birling's speech conveys her manner by being filled with disapproval, reminders of what is proper and decent, and expressions of disgust. Her expressions convey attitudes without necessarily being explicit ('**girls of that class**').

Sheila's speech changes through the play from the rather '**excited**' pretty girl of the opening stage directions who speaks '**gaily**', to a woman of insight, with longer and more articulate speeches.

 Watch an actor explain how she learns her lines on Cambridge Elevate.

### Language and feelings

Priestley conveys his characters' feelings through the use of stage directions such as '**excited**', '**angrily**', '**bitterly**'. He also uses punctuation to indicate **emphasis** in exclamations, questions and repetition. He indicates uncertainty or unwillingness to go further by using dashes. Also, as in all speech, he uses emotive words such as '**awful**' and '**poor girl**' to convey mood by expressing an obvious sentiment.

Sometimes, speech is expressive of mood more by what is not said explicitly, as in the Inspector's '**Quite so**' when Birling has tried to impress him with his social positions. In cases like these, members of the audience draw their own inferences about meaning.

## Language and the generations

Priestley also characterises the generations by their language habits. For example when Sheila calls Eric '**squiffy**', Mrs Birling comments, '**What an expression, Sheila! Really, the things you girls pick up these days!**'

## Language and status

Language reveals far more than simply information. It can tell you a great deal about the attitudes, ideas and relationships that lie behind the language the character uses. On the other hand, it can be used simply as a short cut to indicating status. For example Edna has only four lines in the play. This is one of them:

Please, sir, an inspector's called.

If Edna mattered in the play as a person, her speech may indicate feeling and attitude. What would be the effect if she was shown to have an attitude as in the examples below?

- Informal and relaxed: 'Hi, there's an inspector looking for you.'
- Offhand and irritated: 'Hey, someone's at the door. Says he's an inspector or something.'
- Aloof and higher status: 'Listen. There's an inspector at the door. Come here, immediately.'

 **Watch some actors discussing Edna's lines on Cambridge Elevate.**

Even in a simple speech like this, each word that Edna uses tells us a great deal. By beginning the speech with '**Please**', for example, she is immediately showing that she is a little nervous about interrupting and is of a lower status. She calls Birling '**Sir**', showing respect to him as her employer.

In Edna's case, the language is not intended to indicate anything of her thoughts or feelings or personality. Her speech is intended to do no more than match her function as a servant. This is where it differs from the speech of other characters in the play.

## DEVELOP AND REVISE

### Present the characters

1. Work in pairs. Discuss the opening stage directions and how Priestley suggests a director should present each of the characters. Think about the 'realism' of the play, and the language used. For example:

   a. the '*provincial*' tone of Birling: what sort of regional accent should he have to show he is from the 'provinces' rather than London?
   
   b. the authoritative tone of the Inspector: should he speak in a regional accent or use a neutral accent?
   
   c. the '*excited*' nature of Sheila at the beginning of the play and whether you think she should share her father's accent or (like Eric) speak differently because of his public school and university education?
   
   d. Should Mrs Birling, described as her husband's '*social superior*', have an accent very different from his?

2. Find examples of where Priestley uses punctuation and shorter or longer sentences or speeches, to convey characters and show how they change throughout the play.

3. Find three quotations from different characters at the beginning, middle and end of the play. Work in pairs and take it in turns to be interviewed about the meaning of the language in each quotation.

4. When you have finished your interviews, choose the most successful one and write a short paragraph about the use of language in that quotation, using the ideas you have discussed.

# 15 Language

## What an expression, Sheila!

*Mrs Birling: Act Two*

## Characters and language

Look at the following list of words describing the type of language you might hear in a play.

- authoritative
- slang
- juvenile
- misleading
- evasive
- snobbish
- stressed and desperate
- self-confident
- guarded
- respectful/deferential
- contemptuous
- supportive
- emphatic
- pleading
- confused
- polite
- irritated
- pleased
- flattering
- hesitant/doubtful

**1** Work in small groups. Copy and complete the following table to identify how Priestley uses language to present his characters.

| Character | Language | Supporting detail (quotation) | What the audience understands and interprets |
|---|---|---|---|
| Birling | bullying, self-promoting | 'Why you hysterical young fool – get back – or I'll –' | Birling insults his son and threatens physical violence. |
| Sheila | | | |
| Edna | | | |
| Mrs Birling | | | |
| Eric | | | |
| Gerald | | | |
| the Inspector | | | |

# Preparing for your exam

Your progress in this unit:
- understand what the exam requires and the skills you need to show
- prepare for your exam by planning and responding to a practice question
- assess your skills against example responses to the question
- improve your skills in writing for GCSE English Literature.

## What the exam requires

For your GCSE English Literature, you will be assessed on *An Inspector Calls* in **Section A** of **Paper 2: Modern texts and poetry**. You will have 2 hours and 15 minutes to complete Paper 2 and it is worth 60% of your GCSE English Literature.

You will have to answer **one** essay question from a choice of two on *An Inspector Calls*. This question is worth 30 marks. Four marks are also available for AO4 on this question.

## What to do in the exam

- At the beginning of the exam, spend some time looking carefully at the question. Make sure you understand exactly what you are being asked to do.
- Make notes before you answer the question, so you are prepared. You could make a spider diagram or list.
- Remember to use quotations as evidence.
- Remember to check over your work when you have finished.

## The assessment objective skills

For this question, your answers will be assessed against four assessment objectives (AOs) – skills that you are expected to show. These are shown in full in the Introduction and outlined below in relationship to your responses. Notice the marks for each assessment objective and take account of this as you manage your time and focus your response.

- **AO1:** Read, understand and write about what happens in the play, referring to the text and using relevant quotations (12 marks).
- **AO2:** Analyse the language, form and structure used by Priestley to create meanings and effects (12 marks).
- **AO3:** Show an understanding of the context of the play. This might include, depending on the question, when Priestley wrote the play, the period in which he set the play and why, its relevance to audiences then and to you in the 21st century (6 marks).
- **AO4:** Use a range of vocabulary and sentence structures for clarity, purpose and effect, with accurate spelling and punctuation (4 marks).

# Planning and responding to a question

Read the following practice questions and the student's plan for a response to question 1. Remember: in the exam you will respond to either question 1 or question 2.

## Practice question 1

> How and why does Sheila change in *An Inspector Calls*?
>
> Write about:
>
> - how Sheila responds to her family and to the Inspector
> - how Priestley presents Sheila by the way he writes.
>
> [30 marks]
> AO4 [4 marks]

## Practice question 2

> How does Priestley explore responsibility in *An Inspector Calls*?
>
> Write about:
>
> - the ideas about responsibility in *An Inspector Calls*
> - how Priestley presents these ideas by the way he writes.
>
> [30 marks]
> AO4 [4 marks]

 Complete this assignment on Cambridge Elevate.

# Plan your answer

The following spider diagram shows how you might plan a response to question 1.

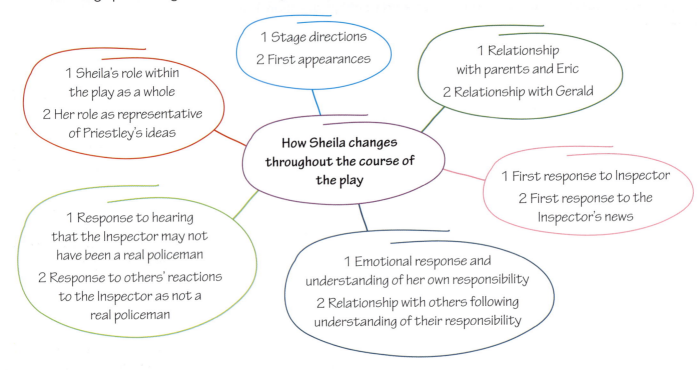

Remember:

## Practice question 1
- ✔ **The best answers** will explore Priestley's craft and purpose in creating the character of Sheila. They will connect what the character does to the writer's ideas and to the effects upon an audience watching. They will offer a personal response and provide many well-explained details.
- ✔ **Good answers** will show a clear understanding of how Priestley develops the character of Sheila, using well-chosen examples.
- ✔ **Weaker answers** will only explain what **happens** to Sheila, without using many examples or mentioning how Priestley presents the character.

## Practice question 2
- ✔ **The best answers** will explore Priestley's craft in presenting ideas. They will connect what the characters say and do to the writer's ideas and to the effects upon an audience watching. They will offer a personal response and provide many well-explained details.
- ✔ **Good answers** will show a clear understanding of how Priestley presents ideas, using well-chosen examples.
- ✔ **Weaker answers** will only explain ideas in the play without using many examples or mentioning how Priestley presents them.

# Preparing for your exam

## Showing your skills

To help you think about your own writing, look at these six example paragraphs of writing about *An Inspector Calls*. The annotations show the range of skills displayed in each paragraph.

---

Sheila is Mr and Mrs Birling's daughter. She is engaged to Gerald.

*Some simple facts stated.*

---

Sheila is pleased to be engaged to Gerald and proud of the engagement ring he gave her: 'It's wonderful … Isn't it a beauty?'

*Statement supported with quotation.*

---

Priestley shows her happy because she has got engaged: 'It's perfect. Now I really feel engaged.' But he mentioned before this that Gerald had not seen her much last summer, so the audience may think there was something behind this that may turn out to be important.

*Explanation structured by reference to author, audience and other parts of the text.*

---

Priestley makes her seem naïve and trusting at the beginning, and a bit immature. She calls her mother and father 'Mummy' and 'Daddy'. Getting engaged is a sign of being grown up, but she doesn't feel engaged until she gets a ring, which is quite immature. Also, she teases her brother by calling him a 'chump' and an 'ass', which is what younger brothers and sisters do.

*Provides a range of detail to keep clearly illustrating a point.*

---

Sheila seems a bit childish at the start because her parents still treat her in a childish way, even though she has just got engaged. Priestley puts in several clues about this as the play goes on. For example Mrs Birling says 'The things you girls pick up these days' and Birling accuses the Inspector of 'upsetting the child'. This suggests she has been brought up in an over-protected way, so that she is not ready to face up to life outside the family. The way she reacts to the news about Eva Smith shows that she grows up fast, and also sees what's wrong with the protected life her parents have built around her.

*Uses details to develop an interpretation that goes beyond what the text states explicitly.*

---

Priestley uses Sheila to contrast with her parents, who are secure in their wealth and status (Birling has been a mayor and a magistrate) and feel no responsibility for life outside the family and the business. She becomes someone who recognises the need for a wider sense of belonging to the human race. This means setting aside values based on business and profit and accepting all people as equal in need for respect: 'They are not cheap labour – they're people.' This is made dramatically visible on stage by her change from simple excited youngster to adviser and critic of her parents, and the way she keeps to her new understanding even when she knows that the Inspector may not have been a real policeman. Unlike her parents, she does not look for excuses to avoid facing the truth that they have learnt from the Inspector.

*An argued interpretation focused on author, theatrical context and ideas.*

## Plan and write your own response

Now plan and write your own response to one of the practice questions. You can then assess your skills against the example responses that follow.

## ASSESS YOUR SKILLS

The following extracts are from sample responses to practice question 1. They provide examples of skills at different levels when writing for GCSE English Literature. Use these examples to assess your own skills in responding to the practice questions, so that you know what you do well and can focus on areas to improve.

Compare these extracts with your own answer to the practice question. As you read the responses, think about how far each example – and your own answer – is successful in:

- using details from the text to support what the students have written
- using details to build up an interpretation of a character or a theme
- exploring Priestley's use of language and structure as well as his intentions in writing the play.

**Student A**

Sheila is the daughter of the Birlings who are a wealthy family. She gets engaged to Gerald Croft, whose family is also wealthy and his father is a Sir. Mr Birling is pleased about her getting engaged because it may lead to the Croft business and his business joining up and 'no longer competing' but 'working together'. So everything starts with them all 'pleased with themselves'. She is really pleased to get an engagement ring: 'it's wonderful – isn't it a beauty?' She's a bit young in the way she behaves, like she calls her parents 'Mummy' and 'Daddy' so you expect her to be a bit of a bubble-head, but she changes when she hears about Eva Smith. Straightaway she feels sorry for what's happened to the girl, even though she doesn't know who it is that she's hearing about. When she realises it was the girl she got sacked, she sees that it was wrong and she feels ashamed.

In this part of the response, Student A engages with the character as a real person, rather than a product of the writer's craft. This shows:

- understanding of character, but not characterisation
- obvious textual detail to support simple comments on character
- awareness of the character's attitude and feeling
- awareness of the character's development
- some awareness of the importance of stage directions.

**Student B**

Priestley shows that Sheila at the start is happy and simple because she is excited by the ring, not just because it is beautiful, but because of how it makes her feel: 'I think it's perfect. Now I really feel engaged', which suggests that just agreeing to get engaged was not enough for her to believe it. I think this is a bit of a juvenile attitude because it's what adults agree between themselves that matters more than a symbol like a ring.

The reason Priestley makes her seem so juvenile early on is to show how much she grows up when she learns what her actions have led to. The audience sees a big difference when she shows a different kind of emotion on behalf of Eva Smith's suffering, which Priestley shows by stage directions and her speech: '(Distressed) Sorry! It's just that I can't help thinking about this girl'. Because she has been shocked by what she has heard, she wants other people to share her feelings. This makes her attack her father's lack of feeling, and stop being his little daughter and instead criticise him: 'They are not cheap labour! They're people'. This is a dramatic change in her character and in her relationship with her father.

In this part of the response, Student B is clearly focused on the author's craft and purpose, and on the text as a drama text. The response engages with character and relationship. It includes personal interpretation. It shows:

- understanding of Priestley's characterisation
- sustained comment on meaning of textual detail
- awareness of effects on the stage and on the audience
- some exploration of her feelings and motives
- effective use of textual detail in stage directions and speech.

## Student C

The play is about the need to go beyond self-interest and survival in order to make a more equal and fair society. Priestley's views are an attack on people who think that business and profit are the main things in life (capitalists) and are based on principles of socialism, which is a way of thinking society is a family bigger than your own family unit, with everyone entitled to equal respect, whatever their wealth or status.

In the play, Mr and Mrs Birling represent the capitalist, selfish point of view, such as 'We need to see that our interests – and the interests of Capital – are properly protected'. At the beginning, Sheila does not have her own point of view. What makes the play dramatically interesting is the way she comes to a view because of what she learns from the Inspector. This makes her challenge her father's way of looking at business and people: 'They're not cheap labour – they're people'. What she learns is that she has been, without knowing it, responsible for events leading up to a girl's death. She is very honest in accepting her responsibility, and thinks that everyone should accept responsibility for their actions, even if they did not know what their actions would lead to.

This is what makes Sheila different from her parents. They try to justify what they did, and don't want to accept that they have anything to do with a young woman who caused trouble through a strike and who seemed to insult the family by using their name. The audience sees this best when the parents try to wriggle out of any responsibility by saying the Inspector is not a real Inspector, probably a Socialist or some sort of a 'crank'. Sheila says, 'You're just beginning to pretend all over again' and that it doesn't matter if the Inspector is real or not because whatever makes people inspect themselves can result in understanding more about yourself and your society.

---

In this part of the response, Student C sets the play in a wider context of relevant ideas. The response presents characters as aspects of the author's purpose in representing ideas, and includes some possible effects upon audiences. It shows:

- developed exploration of the writer's ideas
- a focus on theatre and effects on the audience
- a focus on Sheila's dramatic presentation
- a conceptualised response
- well-used textual detail.

Use what you have learnt from this section to focus on skills to improve for your examination.

# Planning and responding to a question

Now use what you have learnt to plan and write a response to a further practice question.

## Practice question 1

> How does Priestley present some of the differences between the older and younger generations in *An Inspector Calls*?
>
> Write about:
>
> - how the different generations respond to events and to each other
> - how Priestley presents the different generations in the play.
>
> [30 marks]
> AO4 [4 marks]

## Practice question 2

> What do you think is the importance of the ending of *An Inspector Calls*?
>
> Write about:
>
> - how the ending of the play presents some important ideas
> - how Priestley presents these ideas by the ways he writes.
>
> [30 marks]
> AO4 [4 marks]

Complete this assignment on Cambridge Elevate.

## Showing your skills in your response

Remember that your answers need to cover four assessment objectives – skills that the examiners expect you to show. In pairs, assess the skills in your responses. Answers might include some of the following.

## Practice question 1

**AO1**

- Sheila and Eric's relationship with their parents
- Mr and Mrs Birling's relationships with their grown children and with Gerald
- Sheila, Eric and Gerald's attitudes and manner at the start of the play and later
- Mr and Mrs Birling's attitudes and manner at the start of the play and later.

123

## GCSE English Literature for AQA: An Inspector Calls

### AO2

- comments on use of dialogue, for example questions, answers, hesitations, exclamations
- comments on effects of particular stage directions to indicate movement, manner, tone of voice.

### AO3

- characters' ideas about themselves, their family, their status and the world outside the home
- comparison of attitudes to Eva Smith
- Priestley's ideas and purposes in showing a difference between the generations.

### AO4

- use of a range of vocabulary and sentence structures for clarity, purpose and effect
- accurate spelling and punctuation.

## Practice question 2

### AO1

- ways in which characters have changed/have not changed at the end
- reasons for changing or not changing
- the Inspector's role in presenting other characters with reasons to change.

### AO2

- comments on the use of dialogue, for example questions, answers, evasions, acceptance, denial
- comments on the effects of particular stage directions to indicate motive, feeling or attitude.

### AO3

- ideas about partnership in marriage, for example Sheila and Gerald, Mr and Mrs Birling
- ideas about individuals and society
- comparison of characters' responses to the Inspector's information and questions
- Priestley's ideas about community and responsibility.

### AO4

- use of a range of vocabulary and sentence structures for clarity, purpose and effect
- accurate spelling and punctuation.

Preparing for your exam

> *As they stare guiltily and dumbfounded, the curtain falls.*
>
> Stage direction: Act Three

# Glossary

**adaptation** a text that has been changed from one form to another – for example from a play into a film

**character** a person in a story; even when based on real people, characters in plays or novels are invented or fictionalised

**characterisation** the techniques a writer uses to describe characters and make them seem real

**cliff-hanger** the end of an episode or an instalment when something surprising happens, so people will want to find out what happens next

**climax** the high point and most dramatic moment in a scene, act or play

**context** the historical circumstances of a piece of writing, which affect what an author wrote and the way they wrote it

**denouement** the final part of a play, when all the strands of the plot are drawn together and resolved

**dialogue** a conversation between two or more characters in a novel, play or film

**documentary** a film that uses pictures or interviews with people involved in real events to provide a report on a subject; documentaries can contain opinion, but they should be based on facts and evidence.

**dramatic irony** when the audience knows something that a character on stage is unaware of

**emphasis** the extra force given to a word or phrase when a writer wants it to make a particular impact

**exposition** a detailed explanation of a situation or event

**expression** the way that a word or phrase is spoken to show feeling or emotion

**first person** a way of writing that tells a story through the eyes of one of the characters, using the pronouns 'I', 'my' and 'me'

**monologue** a long speech given by a character in a play to another character or characters

**rhetorical question** a question intended to make a point rather than requiring an answer

**screenplay** a script for a film

**setting** the description of the place in which a story is set

**stereotype** an oversimplified but common image or idea of a particular person or thing

**storyboard** a sequence of drawings that show the different scenes in a story.

**subtext** the unspoken thoughts and motives of a character in a play or novel

**turning points** in any drama, characters have important moments in which their character changes or develops; these key moments are referred to as 'turning points'

**well-made play** a genre of play that follows a carefully constructed plot, often based on a secret that is revealed at the climax

# Acknowledgements

Permission has been granted by United Artists on behalf of the Estate of the late J.B. Priestley to reproduce extracts from *An Inspector Calls*.

## Picture credits

cover Hirz/Archive Photos/Getty Images; p. 6 49006785/Fotolia; p. 8 Joan Marcus/ArenaPAL/Topfoto; p. 13 Alastair Muir/Rex Features; pp. 14–15 Donald Cooper/Photostage; p. 16 bizoo_n/Fotolia; p. 17 Lovelace/Rex Features; p. 19 diamondart/Fotolia; p. 23 AF Archive/Alamy; p. 24 kasto80/Thinkstock; p. 25 Donald Cooper/Photostage; p. 27 theatrepix/Alamy; p. 29 serggn/Fotolia; p. 32 Photos.com/Thinkstock; p. 33 Topical Press Agency/Thinkstock; p. 35 theatrepix/Alamy; p. 39 (t) Everett Historical/Shutterstock; p. 39 (b) rus09/Shutterstock; p. 40 Donald Cooper/Photostage; p. 41 Lauri Wiberg/Thinkstock; p. 43 Francis Loney/ArenaPAL/Topfoto; p. 44 AF Archive/Alamy; p. 48 Ysbrand Cosijn/Thinkstock; p. 49 theatrepix/Alamy; p. 50 Aleks_ei/Fotolia; p. 53 stokkete/Fotolia; p. 56 Argus/Fotolia; p. 57 theatrepix/Alamy; p. 60 Sheila Burnett/ArenaPAL/Topfoto; p. 63 Donald Cooper/Photostage; p. 64 Martin Pietak/Thinkstock; p. 65 Pete Jones/ArenaPAL/Topfoto; p. 69 Pete Jones/ArenaPAL/Topfoto; p. 70 Donald Cooper/Photostage; p. 72 Olivier Le Queinec/Shutterstock; p. 73 Marilyn Kingwill/ArenaPAL/Topfoto; p. 75 Netfalls - Remy Musser/Shutterstock; p. 76 John Vickers/University of Bristol Theatre Collection/ArenaPAL; p. 80 Jerry Sliwowski/Fotolia; p. 81 Henrietta Butler/ArenaPAL/Fotolia; p. 82 Henrietta Butler/ArenaPAL/Topfoto; p. 84 Donald Cooper/Photostage; p. 88 theatrepix/Alamy; p. 89 Donald Cooper/Photostage; p. 91 brat82/Fotolia; p. 92 Donald Cooper/Photostage; p. 96 Bettina Strenske; p. 98 Joan Marcus/ArenaPAL/Topfoto; p. 101 Joan Marcus/ArenaPAL/Topfoto; p. 103 John Vickers/University of Bristol Theatre Collection/ArenaPAL/Topfoto; p. 104 UPP/Topfoto; p. 107 John Vickers/University of Bristol Theatre Collection/ArenaPAL/Topfoto; p. 108 Donald Cooper/Photostage; p. 112 Donald Cooper/Photostage; p. 113 Francis Loney/ArenaPAL/Topfoto; p. 115 Donald Cooper/Photostage; p. 116 Pete Jones/ArenaPAL/Topfoto; p. 125 Donald Cooper/Photostage.

Produced for Cambridge University Press by

White-Thomson Publishing
www.wtpub.co.uk

Project editor: Sonya Newland
Designer: Kim Williams, 320 Media